Literary Amazonia

Florida A&M University, Tallahassee
Florida Atlantic University, Boca Raton
Florida Gulf Coast University, Ft. Myers
Florida International University, Miami
Florida State University, Tallahassee
University of Central Florida, Orlando
University of Florida, Gainesville
University of North Florida, Jacksonville
University of South Florida, Tampa
University of West Florida, Pensacola

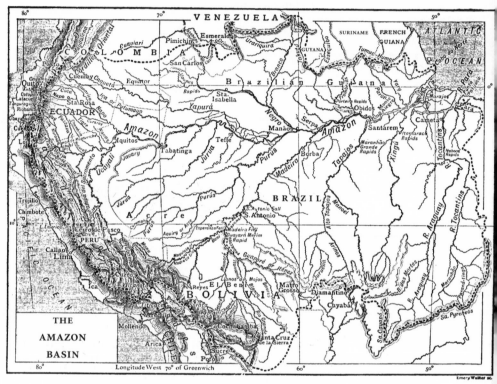

Map of the Amazon basin. Based on a 1911 map in the *Encyclopaedia Britannica*, eleventh edition, copyright 1911, p. 785.

Literary Amazonia

Modern Writing by Amazonian Authors

edited by Nicomedes Suárez-Araúz

University Press of Florida

Gainesville · Tallahassee · Tampa · Boca Raton

Pensacola · Orlando · Miami · Jacksonville · Ft. Myers

09 08 07 06 05 04   6 5 4 3 2 1

Library of Congress Cataloging-in-Publication Data
Literary Amazonia: modern writing by Amazonian authors /
edited by Nicomedes Suárez-Araúz.
p. cm.
Includes bibliographical references.
ISBN 0-8130-2728-4 (cloth: alk. paper)
1. Brazilian literature—Amazon River Region—History and criticism.
2. Colombian literature—Amazon River Region—History and criticism.
3. Peruvian literature—Amazon River Region—History and criticism.
4. Brazilian literature—20th century—History and criticism. 5. Colombian literature—20th century—History and criticism. 6. Peruvian literature—20th century—History and criticism. I. Poeta Movima, 1946-
PQ9691.A494L58 2004
869.09'9811'0904—dc22   2003070508

The University Press of Florida is the scholarly publishing agency for the
State University System of Florida, comprising Florida A&M University,
Florida Atlantic University, Florida Gulf Coast University, Florida International University, Florida State University, University of Central Flor-
ida, University of Florida, University of North Florida, University
of South Florida, and University of West Florida.

University Press of Florida
15 Northwest 15th Street
Gainesville, FL 32611-2079
http://www.upf.com

To Kristine, my light of affection, for three decades my fellow traveler
through Amazonia, and to our sons Niquito and Andrés, lovingly

To Thiago de Mello and my fellow writers and artists
of the Amazon basin,
with admiration and friendship,
and to my colleague Charles Cutler, steadfast and dear friend

Contents

List of Illustrations   ix
Acknowledgments   xi
Introduction   1

Poetry

Raúl Otero Reiche (1906–1976)   22
Violeta Branca (1915–2000)   24
Julio de la Vega (1924–)   27
Max Martins (1926–)   29
Thiago de Mello (1926–)   33
Luiz Bacellar (1928–)   38
Jorge Tufic (1930–)   41
Germán Lequerica Perea (1931–)   44
Jacqueline de Weever (1932–)   47
Alcides Werk (1934–)   48
Astrid Cabral (1936–)   51
Elson Farias (1936–)   54
João de Jesus Paes Loureiro (1939–)   58
Fernando Urbina Rangel (1939–)   62
César Calvo (1940–2000)   64
Pedro Shimose (1940–)   67
Anibal Beça (1946–)   71
Nicomedes Suárez-Araúz (1946–)   75
Los Escribanos de Loén (1946–)   80
Sui-Yun (1955–)   82
Juan Carlos Galeano (1958–)   84
Ana Varela Tafur (1963–)   88
Yenny Muruy Andoque (1969–)   90

Prose

Alfredo Flores (1900–1987) 96
Ciro Alegría (1909–1967) 100
Benjamin Sanches (1915–1978) 106
Erasmo Linhares (1934–) 109
Astrid Cabral (1936–) 112
José Balza (1939–) 115
César Calvo (1940–2000) 118
Max Carphentier (1945–) 146
Márcio Souza (1946–) 149
Nicomedes Suárez-Araúz (1946–) 164
Milton Hatoum (1952–) 169
Homero Carvalho Oliva (1957–) 173

Biographies 179

Illustrations

Frontispiece. Map of the Amazon Basin

1. View of the landscape across the San Mateo River,
on the road from Cochabamba to Moxos, Bolivia   21

2. *A Lenda da Mãe do Rio*
[Legend of the Mother of the River] (1989)   95

3. *A Lenda da Tocandira* [The Legend of the Tocandira] (1980)   178

Acknowledgments

To all the authors who contributed to this anthology we express our deep gratitude. We also owe a special debt of gratitude to the superb translators who, despite their multiple commitments, so generously gave of themselves to the project.

I warmly thank Charles Cutler, a dear friend and colleague at Smith College, and R. Kelly Washbourne, for their steadfast and magnanimous contributions. I extend my thanks to Smith College's Spanish and Portuguese Department for its kind support, and particularly to former president John M. Connolly, provost/dean of the faculty Susan Bourque and deans Don Baumer and Charles Staelin, for providing funding that allowed me to do research in Amazonia.

I am grateful to Rainer Schulte, founder of American Literary Translators Association, and to Antonio Benítez-Rojo for their encouragement and friendship.

I feel fortunate that my travels through the countries of the Amazon basin brought me into contact with extraordinary persons. Their contributions as members of the advisory board of the Center for Amazonian Literature and Culture (CALC) were extremely valuable, and the resulting friendships have been invaluable. Among them, Thiago de Mello, Anibal Beça, João de Jesus Paes Loureiro, and Márcio Souza spontaneously offered their help in contacting other writers from Brazilian Amazonia. Likewise, Beatriz Alzate, of the Universidad de los Andes, and her colleagues Fernando Urbina Rangel, Enrique Pérez, and Betty Osorio, in Colombia, and José Balza, in Venezuela, guided me in my search for writers. I am equally grateful to the citizens of Iquitos, Peru, Joaquín García Sánchez, director of the Centro de Estudios Teológicos de la Amazonia, Alejandra Schindler, director of the CETA's Biblioteca Amazónica of Iquitos, and Ana Varela Tafur, one of Peru's foremost poets. I extend my thanks to Juan Botasso Boetti and José Juncosa, directors of the Abya-Yala publishing house of

Quito, for their advice. A special thanks to Candace Slater, director of the Townsend Center for the Humanities at the University of California, Berkeley, for her gracious support.

I am grateful to several of my Bolivian compatriots with whom I have had instructive conversations about Bolivian culture, among them the important cultural figures José Luis Roca García, Alcides Parejas, Marcelo Araúz Lavadenz, and Arnaldo Lijerón Casanovas. I extend a special thanks to Mário Ypiranga Monteiro, to Tenório Telles, and to the owners of Editora Valer of Manaus for providing valuable information on writers and the culture of their region. We will always remember with gratitude the generous collaboration of the late and distinguished man of letters of Manaus, Paulo Jacob.

We are most grateful to the celebrated artist Moacir Andrade for granting us permission to reproduce his work. We extend our thanks to Marian MacDonald, director of the Jacobsen Center of Smith College, for her editorial assistance, to Lisa Carta, for her expertise in composing graphic images for this book, and to Lindsey Benitz and Laurel Damashek, editorial assistants at CALC.

Introduction

Toward a Pan-Amazonian Literary Vision

One can speak of "Amazonian literature" in the same sense in which
one speaks of Peruvian, Chilean, Bolivian, Cuban, or other literatures.
Luis Hernán Ramírez

It wasn't until 1940 that people began speaking of
"Amazonian literature" as a convenient way of grouping writers.
Mário Ypiranga Monteiro

The present anthology is a selection of contemporary poetry, short stories, and passages from novels by authors from the regions of the Amazon Basin.[1] This collection draws from the compilation of Amazonian writers that we have carried out at the Center for Amazonian Literature and Culture (CALC), a center founded by Professor Charles Cutler and me in 1993 at Smith College, in Northampton, Massachusetts. One of CALC's central objectives is to collect and promote the writings of Amazonian authors, a category that has been ignored. The present collection, we hope, will spur a reevaluation of the contribution by Amazonian writers to Latin American literature.

Until the twentieth century, definitions of Amazonian writing were based on a textual tradition that was primarily the work of outsiders. Written in Portuguese and Spanish, initially the texts tended to emulate European literary styles. At the same time, that literature, attempting to represent the new and complex reality of the region, was syncretic and hybrid: it superimposed and mixed diverse foreign and native cultural codes. The Indigenous culture and oral literary traditions existed in those writings to the extent to which their authors chose to represent or vindicate the native presence.[2]

A brief review of approaches to the literary history of the region illustrates the outsider and Eurocentric view of Amazonian culture. Some Spanish American critics have equated the earlier modern writing of the area with "la novela de la selva" [the novel of the jungle], a label that sometimes incongruously conflates Spanish-, Portuguese-, and English-language works and includes several genres. For example, Lydia León de Hazera in her book *La novela de la selva hispanoamericana* (1971) lists, besides novels, the travelogues *De Bogotá al Atlántico* (1897) by Santiago Pérez Triana and *The Sea and the Jungle* (1912) by Henry Major Tomlinson, as well as the short-story collections *Inferno verde* (1908) by the Brazilian Alberto Rangel (1871–1945) and *La venganza del cóndor* (1924) by Ventura García Calderón. Except for Ciro Alegría (1909–1967), born in Huamachuco, Peru, the authors León de Hazera mentions are not native to the region. To claim Amazonian "citizenship" for foreign writers such as W. H. Hudson or H. M. Tomlinson would be equivalent to labeling Joseph Conrad an African writer, or E. M. Forster an Indian author.

Following similar criteria, we can speak of "la poesía de la selva" [the poetry of the jungle], or, more comprehensively, group all genres together as "la escritura de la selva hispanoamericana" [the writing of the Spanish American jungle]. These classifications are based on a simplistic notion: "la selva" (from the Latin "silva," meaning "wild" or "savage") manifests a commonplace view of a barbaric social milieu, the product of a hostile natural environment. To be precise, however, the 7 million square kilometers of Amazonia (an area approximately the size of the continental United States) overflow the limits of the jungle: the region spans savannahs, ascends into the sierra, and, at its western limits, falls within the perimeters of Andean cities such as Quito and La Paz. Moreover, within the Amazonian region there are large urban centers, and the population of the region, according to a 1992 UNESCO report, is approximately 23 million, 98 percent of which is ethnically and culturally *mestizo*. These facts seemingly belie the older view of Amazonia as being fundamentally a jungle environment inhabited by a scant Indigenous population. Given the urbanization of several areas of the Basin, it is not surprising that since the 1930s some Amazonian writing has transcended the themes of earlier writings.

It may seem self-evident that Amazonian literature exists. After all, it has a *patria*, a homeland. But the region is made up of territories from several countries—Bolivia, Brazil, Colombia, Ecuador, Peru, and Venezuela—and it also extends into Guyana, Suriname (formerly colonies of England and Holland respectively), and French Guiana, which is still a colonial territory of France. Nonetheless, the social and cultural commonality of the bioregion is remarkable, and it may present a unity greater than that of the diverse Caribbean archipelago and as cohesive as that of the so-called Andean region, which belying its monolithic denomination is made up mostly—66 percent—of Amazonian land. These regions are commonly studied as unified cultures. By contrast, nationalism and insularity have often prevented Amazonians from recognizing their cultural kinship.

Awareness of a similar culture and history spurred the countries of the region to create in 1987 the Union of Amazonian Universities (UNA-MAZ), signaling an impulse toward collaborations, particularly in scientific fields. Since 1975, the year all the nations possessing Amazonian territory signed the Treaty for Amazonian Cooperation, several other such treaties for economic development of Amazonia have been signed. A literary counterpart to this impulse, however, has lagged behind. The publication of CALC's *Amazonian Literary Review* and *Pan-Amazonia*, the center's bulletin, signaled the first international presentation of a Pan-Amazonian literary vision. *Terra das Águas* [Land of the Waters], an interdisciplinary journal of the Nucleus for Amazonian Studies at the Federal University of Brasília, also aims to present aspects of the whole region. A single-issue journal, *Unamazônia* (June 1998), resulted from the first Forum Pan-Amazônico de Cultura, Educação e Meio Ambiente in Belém, Pará, a project in which the organizers of the forum, among them the Brazilian Amazonian writers Márcio Souza (1946–) and João de Jesus Paes Loureiro (1939–), invited me to participate in 1997. The Centro de Estudios Teológicos de la Amazonia (CETA) of Iquitos, Peru, headed by Joaquín García Sánchez, and its Biblioteca Amazónica, directed by Alejandra Schindler, have also been active in cultural exchange, particularly with Brazil and Colombia. Similarly, Beatriz Alzate, a professor at the Universidad de los Andes, in Bogotá, organized presentations by Brazilian Amazonian authors in Colombia. The CETA and the publishing house Abya-Yala of Quito, Ecuador, have published many books on Amazonian themes, especially in the fields of anthropology and ethnography.

Before the 1990s, the separation between the Portuguese- and Spanish-speaking regions of the Basin was extraordinary. During most of the twentieth century, authors from either side of the major linguistic divide were unknown to one another. Notable exceptions were the Colombian José Eustasio Rivera (1889–1928) and the Brazilian Alberto Rangel, both of whom are mentioned in literary histories by the Spanish American critics Arturo Torres Rioseco (1939) and Lydia León de Hazera (1971), and by the

Brazilian Pericles Moraes (1959). Rivera and Rangel, however, were not native to Amazonia.

In the last decade, some Amazonians have attempted to establish a cultural dialogue between the Spanish-speaking and Portuguese-speaking areas of the Amazon region. This first Pan-Amazonian anthology expands such dialogue and also includes English-speaking writing from Guyana. It is an appropriate moment to further such a vision since a few Amazonian authors are achieving recognition in countries outside South America. The Brazilians Thiago de Mello (1926–), Alcides Werk (1934–), João de Jesus Paes Loureiro, Márcio Souza, and Milton Hatoum (1952–); the Bolivians Pedro Shimose (1940–) and Nicomedes Suárez-Araúz (1946–); the Peruvians Ciro Alegría, César Calvo (1940–2000), and Sui-Yun (1955–); and the Venezuelan José Balza (1939–) have had books translated into and published in English, German, Italian, or French. The foundational poet Thiago de Mello, in particular, has been an extraordinary cultural ambassador between his country and the rest of Latin America.

The Sociohistorical Context of Amazonian Literature

Ever since 1542, when the Spanish conquistador Francisco de Orellana described in awe the "river-sea" that soon after was given the name of a classical myth, the historical process of Amazonia has seemed irreversible. It cleared the way for the tragic decimation of Indigenous groups, for the erosion and erasure of their cultures brought about by miscegenation and acculturation, and ultimately for the devastation of the region's natural wholeness. Today Amazonia, as we noted above, is predominantly *mestizo*, belying the image of it as terra incognita inhabited by "barbaric" tribes. Yet Orellana's vision of the region as a savage land persists today in the exoticized images of tourism and in the simplistic representations in news and entertainment media. That vision still perpetuates the notion that Amazonia is essentially a natural environment, a view further emphasized in the last three decades by the international attention to the precariousness of the ecological integrity of the Amazon Basin.

In precolonial times there seems to have been a recurrent Amazonian village (to evoke a notion of Antonio Benítez-Rojo from his study of Caribbean culture, *The Repeating Island*). History has accrued variants on it, but some of its basal components persist. The uniformity of the cultural characteristics of Amazonia on the eve of the European invasion was remarkable, as Betty Meggers has noted in reference to the estimated 1,400 ethnic groups extant at the time (Meggers 1971). Sociohistorical developments in the region since the European arrival in 1542 have superimposed two other key series of cycles on its original autochthonous reality. In the seventeenth and eighteenth centuries came the religious missions (mostly Jesuit); in the nineteenth century began the turbulent neocolonial cycles that reached their apotheosis with the Rubber Boom (1860s–1920) and continued throughout the twentieth century. Cinchona, natural latex, cacao, sugarcane, cotton, Brazil nuts, emeralds, wood, cattle, iron, oil, gold, genetic resources, and illegal drugs spell out the signs of neocolonial extractivist practices of the last 140 years that have led to the present ecological crisis and to a continuation of a deleterious economic dependency of the region on international markets. Each of these economic cycles can be analogically viewed, in the terminology of chaos theory, as an *attractor*, or a point of relative structural stability. That is, they were sudden bonanzas, concentrations of capital in a few hands, booms that cyclically exhausted themselves into incoherence and nearly complete dissolution. Each cycle, and especially the longest lasting one, the Rubber Boom, attracted foreign immigrants to the region who were avid for riches. Among them were Spaniards, Portuguese, British, North Americans, Germans, Swiss, French, Italians, Middle Easterners, Africans, Japanese, and some Chinese. Descendants of these immigrants settled in Amazonia, thus adding to the diversity of the region's cultures.

One key element that unifies the geographic and social components of Amazonia is the mute and eloquent presence of the Amazon River and its more than 1,100 tributaries, next to whose banks live the majority of the inhabitants of the region. These waters, multiple and binary, teeming between droughts and floods, spell out the signs of a vast multiethnic, multilingual, and multicultural text. The heterogeneity of the Amazonian text and its fragmented history informs its pluvial cultures. In them, myriads of foreign signs that entered the rivers in canoes, steamboats, and transatlantic ships resulted in cultural expressions that, notwithstanding their diverse origins, reveal the foundational Indigenous presence. From the juxtaposition of cultural codes, of social and historical circumstances, emerges the Amazonian imaginary space that nourishes its written and sometimes carnivalized literary expressions.

In the last three decades, traditional Amazonian towns and cities such as Iquitos in Peru, Leticia in Colombia, Manaus and Belém in Brazil, and Riberalta, Trinidad, and Santa Cruz in Bolivia have been undergoing a transformation into modern and Westernized urban centers. These towns and cities are becoming the new ultra-syncretic centers where Indian religion and lore mingle with Christian practices, where bows and arrows and AK assault rifles are handled by natives, where oxcarts and jets coexist, where cybernauts live side by side with shamans. The postmodern assemblage of cultural signs lends specific inflections to the various river cultures of Amazonia, depending on their ethnic mix and communication with the outside world. Nonetheless, the citizens of the various Amazonian regions have more in common with one another than with the inhabitants of the capital cities, or cities from other geographic regions. Thus, a Bolivian from the Mamoré River may have more in common with a Brazilian from Guajaramirím, Manaus, or Belém than with a countryman from the highland cities of La Paz or Oruro.

Amazonian Literary History

European chroniclers, explorers, and naturalists conceived the first written visions of the region. To them it was either benign or evil, a paradise on earth or a living inferno. Amazonia was either the victim of exploitation or the victimizer of those who ventured to explore it or live in it. Later writers reiterated those visions, giving them their own inflections. They also conceived the region in new metaphors: as lost paradise, green hell, green desert, vortex, chaos, promised land, immature land, green mansions, and green architecture. The anthropologist Claude Lévi-Strauss labeled the region a sad or melancholic tropical land; adventurers, developers, and government bureaucrats see it as the last frontier. On the basis of Amazonia's contribution to the planet's ecological health, international environmentalists have labeled Amazonia "the lungs of the world."

In 1908 Euclides da Cunha, observing the portentous forces of Amazonian nature, particularly of its rivers, which year by year transform the landscape, stated that Amazonia was a land whose history was unstable and self-erasing. His statement also applies to the region's social and historical record, which given the limited archeological research of its origins remains singularly incomplete. Furthermore, historical discourse of the area is dependent, as Neide Gondim and Pedro Maligo have noted, on an inherited and often fabled "discourse handed down in historical and literary texts" (Maligo 1998: 41). Amazonia's collective memory is therefore a puzzle that may never be completed since large segments of the Basin's history disappear even before they are recorded. The perception of the historical lacunae of Amazonia suggested the image of "green plains of amnesia," an image that led me in 1973 to formulate Amnesis, an aesthetic of creative amnesia inspired by the voids in the collective record of my homeland.

The history of modern Amazonian writing remains tentative and fragmentary. In the case of Bolivia, writers from the region did not classify their literary production as Amazonian, perhaps because of political rivalry with Brazil or because they chose—echoing Domingo Faustino Sarmiento's dialectic—to shun the stigma of the purported barbarism attributed to the region. Yet the label, as I have argued elsewhere, is more precise than *escritores orientales* or *del trópico*. The former simply points to a geographic position—eastern—in relation to the Andean centers of power, especially La Paz, the capital city; the other—"tropical"—is a climatologic and ecological appellative. *Amazonian* denotes a specific geo-cultural identification and a historical destiny. In the face of the persistent vanishing of cultural elements of the region, our identification as Amazonian writers does not negate our citizenship of our respective countries; rather it signals a desire to vindicate regions that within national projects of the Basin's countries have remained forsaken and forgotten as fundamental components of those countries.

Questioning the existence and setting the parameters of Brazilian Amazonian writing, Mário Ypiranga Monteiro has noted that it was not until 1940 that the term began to be used as a convenient way of grouping writers. Modern Amazonian literature in Brazil began with the publication in 1819 of an epic poem, *A Muhuraida*, by the Portuguese writer Henrique João Wilkens (eighteenth century), a work that Márcio Souza has labeled "a poetry of genocide" since it glorifies the decimation of the Mura Indians (Souza 1998: 136). Another foundational poem, *Cobra Norato* (1931) by Raul Bopp (1898–1984), also an outsider to Amazonia, is representative of the celebrated anthropophagic aesthetics of Brazil's Modernist movement of the 1920s, whose aims to realize a break from the past had more in common with Anglo-American Modernism than with Spanish American *Modernismo*, which was influenced by Parnassian and Symbolist writings. The anthropophagic aesthetics propounded by Oswaldo de Andrade (1890–1954) in 1928, and embodied by Bopp's work, propose the use of native cultural materials and the absorption of foreign cultural elements by means of parodic cannibalization, a singular critical attitude in Latin America that skirts the aporia of cultural self-definition on the face of foreign influences. Following Andrade's precepts, Bopp practiced an exemplary adoption of the Indigenous imaginary, an adoption that has been emulated by such Amazonian writers as Violeta Branca (1915–2000), Jorge Tufic (1930–), Elson Farias (1936–), João de Jesus Paes Loureiro, and Márcio Souza, among others.

In Bolivia, as in Peru, writing from the Amazonian regions has, with a certain lag, followed the literary movements of the rest of Spanish America: from Modernismo to Posmodernismo (1880s–1920) to the inclusion of avant-garde currents (in Amazonia, since the 1930s). However, in a recent literary history of Peru, the stages of Peruvian Amazonian writing are periodized, significantly, in relation to key economic cycles: Período Cauchero [Rubber Boom period] (1860s–1920); Post-Cauchero [Post–Rubber Boom] (1921–1970); and Petrolero [Oil Exploration period] (1970–1991) (Toro Montalvo 1996: 93). By using this framework, César Toro Montalvo suggests that Amazonian literature in his country has no autonomy from economic developments: neocolonial extractivism conditions its periodization.

In Colombia, Ecuador, and Venezuela, the other Spanish-speaking countries in the Amazonian Basin, writing by native Amazonians is exiguous. In Amazonia's Colombia it was not until the 1980s that literary creations began to appear. Because of his dedication as a researcher and prolonged living in the region, Fernando Urbina Rangel (1939–) could be classified as Amazonian. Juan Carlos Galeano (1958–) and Yenny Muruy Andoque (1969–) are among the few writers who, in the last two decades of the twentieth century, have emerged from the region. Ecuador presents a singular case in that the scanty urbanization of its Amazonian region has yet to produce a single published writer born in that area. Venezuela has the distinction of having a fringe of Amazonian territory and also a section that corresponds to the Orinoco Valley. The culture of the Orinoco region tends to be a mixture of Antillean and Amazonian culture, with the former being predominant in that river's delta. Nonetheless, in this anthology we are including the most representative fiction writer from the Orinoco, José Balza.

Like all regional literature, that of Amazonia began centered on the motifs and themes suggested by its natural and social environment. Raúl Otero Reiche (1906–1976) from Bolivia voiced the ancient idea that the telluric is the power that inevitably determines the "social psychology" of human beings. The notion of Amazonian societies as earth-centered was reiterated by Socorro Santiago in 1986: "From the river and the forest, [an Amazonian] takes what is necessary for the sustenance of his body." This environment, she adds, "gigantic and mysterious, . . . impresses on his nervous system strange images, products of fear, fruit of his solitude" (Santiago 1986: 27).

Similarly, the *Enciclopédia de literatura brasileira* states: "Nature, which in Amazonia is at the same time terror, beauty, and magic, explains the lyric vocation and the mystic tendency of Amazonians. . . . The character of the inhabitant of the plains derives from the saturation of his own anxiety. Caught between his two terrible melancholies, that of the river and that of the forest, he turns inward, and withdrawing into self-searching he escapes to a cosmic reality by means of the imagination which invents myths and legends, phantoms, talismans, terrors, demons, superstitions—the whole enchantment of the *caboclos'* [the preferred spelling of the term being *caboco*] collection of fables of the Green Hell" (Coutinho and Sousa 1990: 207).

Whereas sea dwellers live in the midst of the heartbeat of waters that speak in the plural, the river dweller lives in the apparent monochord of a Heraclitean flow. The rivers' binary rhythm of droughts and floods seems to be that flow's only variant. Naturally, the urban dweller of cities such as Manaus or Belém is not as affected as the rural or jungle dweller who lives by the waters and, to a large extent, from them. Considering the omnipresence of the river, Socorro Santiago sees elemental water as the unifying theme in her study of *poetas amazonenses* [poets from Brazil's State of Amazonas] entitled *Uma poética das águas* [A Poetics of the Waters], which she appropriately grounds in Bachelardian phenomenology.

In the writings presented in this volume, the presence of the region's Indigenous cultures surfaces often mediated by the *caboco*, or mestizo dominant culture, in a distinctive "imaginário amazônico" [Amazonian imaginary space] about which poet João de Jesus Paes Loureiro writes in *Cultura Amazônica: Uma poética do imaginario* [Amazonian Culture: A Poetics of the Imaginary] (1995). Here in our selection we visit the imaginary space that fuses past with present, and that speaks through myth (the language of the individual and collective psyche). Thus, the living myth of the *boto*, the pink river dolphin capable of metamorphosis into human form and interaction with humans, surfaces in the poems of the Brazilians Jorge Tufic, Astrid Cabral (1936–), and Paes Loureiro. Tufic also treats the theme of Jurupari, a polysemic Indigenous figure that mediates and interconnects the human and natural realms. The persistence of the cult of Jurupari, in our days from Guyana to Colombia and Brazil, speaks of the extraordinary vitality of ancient Indigenous culture in the Basin. The reader should be aware, however, that some Amazonian myths are relatively recent or may have changed upon coming in contact with outside cultures. For example, the dolphin cycle, Luíz da Câmara Cascudo notes, probably did not exist among the Indigenous people of precolonial Brazil (Slater 1994: 2).

In his poem "Amazon," the Peruvian César Calvo adapts an Indigenous myth of a most beautiful woman who gave mythogenetic birth to the Amazon River with her inconsolable and torrential weeping. Similarly, we see mythological themes in the poems of the Brazilian Violeta Branca. The sense of the marvelous is also present in the poetry of Elson Farias, who unveils in "Rain Patterns" the mystery and ritual of water and in "The Medicine Man" the miraculous curative powers of a shamanic healer. The shape-shifting qualities attributed to mythic deities are evident in the images of transformation in the poems by Juan Carlos Galeano and Yenny Muruy Andoque, and in my own poems. Jacqueline de Weever (1932–), Farias, Calvo, Urbina Rangel, and Galeano echo in their works Raul Bopp's poetic practice of adapting Indigenous myths and mythic thinking.

A few of the selected poems elicit the myths and realities of the Conquest and El Dorado; others touch on the ensuing colonialism and neocolonialism. Julio de la Vega (1924–) reiterates the image of the jungle vortex that vanquished intruders such as Francisco de Orellana, who, blinded by delusions of incalculable riches, died while attempting to navigate the Amazon River a second time. In "Moxitania" (the land of the Moxos Indians in Bolivia), Pedro Shimose aspires to the Edenic moment that preceded human presence, particularly that of the Europeans. Shimose also evokes the brutish hordes of rubber tappers, many of whom brought, along with their greed, their garish vulgarity and murderous instincts.

This anthology includes more contemporary themes as well, suggesting the impact of modernization on the region. In "Workers" and "Bar do Parque," Paes Loureiro treats the urban theme of dehumanization brought about by capitalist progress. The Bolivian Otero Reiche voices the horrors of the war with Paraguay (1933–1936) that bled his country's Amazonian region. Germán Lequerica Perea (1931–) and Ana Varela Tafur (1963–) refer in a veiled manner to the bloody struggles for social justice in their country, Peru, waged by socialist guerrillas against national government troops. Some of the work by Varela Tafur and Sui-Yun (1955–), a writer of mixed Chinese and Peruvian heritage, exemplifies a confessional tendency in the poetic production of the region. Such a tendency is not exclusive to Peru and is present in poems by several writers from other regions, notably the Brazilians Thiago de Mello and Max Martins (1926–).

The ecological devastation of the region is a central theme in Amazonian poetry. It is treated by the Brazilians Thiago de Mello, Alcides Werk, and Astrid Cabral; by the Colombian Juan Carlos Galeano; and by me, particularly in the cycle of poems entitled *Edible Amazonia* (2002), a bilingual poetry collection in which the Western notions of barbarism commonly applied to Amazonia are subverted by means of irony and parody.

The Amazonian tradition of haiku speaks of the cultural presence for more than a century of a sizable Japanese colony in the Amazon, adding to the vibrant multiculturalism of the region. The adoption of the haiku tradition by Amazonians has its precedent in the poetry of other regions of Brazil and of Spanish America. Luiz Bacellar (1928–), a foundational figure of the modern poetry of Brazil's Amazon region, together with Branca, Martins, Tufic, and Thiago de Mello, initiated, in 1958, haiku writing in Amazonia. Tufic and Anibal Beça (1946–) are two other notable practitioners of that Japanese-inspired poetic tradition.

Amazonian Fiction Writing

The early literary production of the Amazonian region, in poetry as much as in fiction, tended toward an exalted neo-romanticism expressed in a torrential and baroque rhetoric, which in its best pages achieves a memorable lyricism, but which in its worst passages unravels into a commonplace *costumbrismo* (the representation of place in its diverse local manifestations) and an unredeemable thematic *tremendismo* (extreme naturalist thematics). The region's early fiction attempts to document fantastic aspects of an unknown world and tends to transform such aspects "via mythical imagery and the displacement of the writer, into an expression and projection of desire" (Maligo 1998: 152). The environment is a dominant influence over the destiny of humans, but negative social factors are even more determining. This vision leads in the writing of many Amazonian-born authors to a literature of social protest against the dominant classes made up of mestizos, criollos, and Europeans, a protest also directed against foreign intervention in Amazonia's destiny, particularly in the last three decades during which the region has been envisioned in utilitarian terms as a key contributor to the ecological health of the planet. As Pedro Maligo appropriately notes, "The image of Amazonia as the lungs of the world illustrates the issue of how language assumes stronger ideological implications as the displacement of its primary documentary function grows more noticeable. In this organic metaphor, it is clear that the representation of the region has been proposed from an external perspective and that it limits Amazonia to a single mechanical function" (Maligo 1998: 155).

Novels with Amazonian settings written by authors born in the region include foundational works such as *O missionário* [The Missionary] (1891) by Herculano Inglêz de Souza (1853–1918), and *Os Igaraúnas* [The Igaraúnas] (1938) by Raimundo de Morais (1872–1941), an apology against the *Infernista* tradition (a tradition exalting the earlier notion of Amazonia as an infernal land). These works were hardly known outside Brazil.

The Amazonian novel since the 1970s has had a wider international audience, and it has sought to reflect emerging social and historical manifestations. In contemporary novels the telluric themes and motifs of the nineteenth century are still present, together with references to an imaginary space nourished by Indigenous and mestizo or *caboco* lore. The Indian element is particularly evident in the influential polyglossic documentary and mythic fictional work *Las tres mitades de Ino Moxo y otros brujos de la Amazonía* [1981; published in English as *The Three Halves of Ino Moxo* in 1995] by the Peruvian César Calvo. Mixing biographic elements of the life of Medicine Man Don Manuel Córdoba-Ríos or Ino Moxo (born in 1887) with Indigenous myth and lore and ecstatic visions produced by the ingestion of the hallucinogen ayahuasca ("the vine of the soul or death"), Calvo's writings present a critical panorama of Peru's Amazonian and national history, including a scathing condemnation of the abuses and massacres of Indigenous groups perpetrated by the rubber baron Carlos Fermín Fitzcarrald.

Márcio Souza (1946–) is a prolific Brazilian writer and one of the most influential novelists and cultural theorists writing in Portuguese. An ironist, he is the creator of works internationally known for their lively depiction of the Brazilian national character, often featuring a comic flair, a sense of the absurd, and cultural confrontations, especially capitalism invading traditional values. His best-known works, *Galvez: Imperador do Acre* [1977; published in English as *The Emperor of the Amazon*, 1980] and *Mad Maria: Romance* [1980; rendered into English as *Mad Maria*, published in 1985], satirize aspects of the Rubber-Boom history of the region that reflect on contemporary realities, not only in Amazonia but also in Brazil and Latin America in general. Randall Johnson notes: "Souza's works reflect Oswald de Andrade's mordant, satirical sense of humor, which transmits a highly critical political vision of Brazil. . . . Souza's subsequent novels relate political themes—coup d'etat, counterinsurgency, terrorism, international espionage (e.g., *A ordem do dia* [1983; *The Order of the Day*, 1986]), and detective fiction with the literary thriller" (Stern 1988: 328).

In 1989 Milton Hatoum launched a successful literary career with his first novel, *Relato de um certo oriente* [published in English as *The Tree of the Seventh Heaven*, 1994]. Hatoum's novels treat the theme of Lebanese immigration to Amazonia in a heterophonic narrative approach that superbly embodies the nomadic identity construction of his characters. As Marguerite Itamar Harrison notes: "Through the multiplicity of voice, race, and homelands, Hatoum expertly conveys the often-painful incongruities that we confront as immigrants . . ." (2001). Calvo and Hatoum are represented in this selection by passages from their book-length works *Ino Moxo* and *The Tree of the Seventh Heaven*, respectively.

The stories "La llamada" [The Call] by Ciro Alegría and "A caligrafia de Deus" [God's Handwriting] by Márcio Souza present two fundamental poles of Amazonian fiction: the earlier rural, regional writing that achieved its apogee with the "novela de la selva" [novel of the jungle], of which Alegría is an outstanding representative author, and the urban-centered Amazonian writing from the 1980s and beyond. Alegría's story treats the theme of the interrelation between humans and nature. Souza's work depicts the most discernible direction human Amazonia took in the last two decades of the twentieth century. In Souza's Manaus, urbanized Indians become tragic statistical ciphers. One of the two protagonists, Izabel, daughter of a Baniwa Indian father and a Tukano Indian mother, symbolically displays in her mouth the very vortex that devoured her cultural inheritance and dignity. Toothless, wearing grotesque, ill-fitting dentures in an attempt to emulate the idealized images of Caucasian movie stars, she abandons the sphere of her own culture and people and enters into the straight-line labyrinth of degradation into poverty and inevitable prostitution and a senseless death.

The Amazonian short-story tradition had its beginnings in the *quadros de costumbres* (in Spanish, *cuadros de costumbres*) [sketches of customs]. The first important collection in that genre, *Quadros paraenses* [Sketches of Customs of Pará] by José Veríssimo (1857–1916), a Brazilian critic and novelist, was published in 1876. Veríssimo's work is noteworthy for including the first literary manifestations of the tragedy of the rubber gatherers (the *seringueiros*); for the motif of the jungle—or elements of it—as a living organism, even human or superhuman; for the recovery of the myth of the *boto* (the pink river dolphin); and for awakening interest in the poor and humble people (Walther 1948: 43–47). Similar to Veríssimo's *quadros* are those by the Peruvian Amazonian writer Jenaro E. Herrera (1861–1941), *Leyendas y tradiciones de Loreto* [Legends and Traditions of Loreto] (1918). Herrera's work is particularly reminiscent of *Tradiciones peruanas* [Peruvian Traditions], a celebrated collection of short historical anecdotes by Ricardo Palma (1833–1919). Luis Hernán Ramírez notes that Herrera's writings mark in Peru "the birth of Amazonian literature as such, and are the point of departure for a new vein of the short story" akin to what has become known as "magic realism" (Ramírez 1998: 127). The critic Ricardo Vírhuez affirms that the Amazonian author Humberto del Águila (1893–1970) was the founder of the modern Peruvian short story. Fifteen of Águila's stories were published in 1958 in Madrid in a volume entitled *Cuentos amazónicos* [Amazonian Short Stories] (Rodríguez 2000: 3–4). In Bolivia, the modern Amazonian short-story tradition begins with *Desierto verde* [Green Desert] (1933), a collection by Alfredo Flores (1900–1987).

Like longer Amazonian fiction, the contemporary short story has tended to reflect historical, economic, and social developments in the region. Alfredo Flores's story "El sargento Charupás" [Sergeant Charupás] is set in the frontier days during the beginnings of Bolivia's war with Paraguay (1932–1935), a time of strife spurred on by foreign oil companies. This war decimated the youth of Bolivia's Amazonia, who were forcefully enlisted in the war effort. Flores's narrative, which antedates by two decades Juan Rulfo's stories in *El llano en llamas* [The Burning Plain] (1953), shares with Rulfo's certain elements such as sparse description and dialogue interspersed with internal monologue, to suggest the impending tragic resolution of the story's conflict. The narrative "Beri-Beri" [Beriberi] by Erasmo Linhares (1934–) harks back to Brazil's *literatura da borracha* [literature of the Rubber Boom], epitomized by works from the first quarter of the twentieth century, especially Alberto Rangel's short-story collection *Inferno verde* [Green Hell] (1908) from Brazil, and José Eustasio Rivera's novel *La vorágine* [The Vortex] (1924) from Colombia. "Beriberi" parallels thematic aspects of Rangel's short story "Maibi" from *Inferno verde*: in a fit of jealousy, rubber collectors murder their wives who, through no fault of their own but rather because of their families' indentured situation, fall prey to the sexual desire of the owners of the rubber enterprises on which they depend for their livelihood.

The stories "O estropiado" [the cripple] by Benjamin Sanches (1915–

1978) and "Historia de um grão de feijão" [The Story of a Bean] by Astrid Cabral were published in 1963 in books entitled *O outro e outros contos* and *Alameda*, respectively. Antônio Paulo Graça notes that these collections represent a break from the regional-naturalist tendency in the fiction of Brazil's Amazonian region (Graça 1998: 11). Another example of this tendency is the poetic fantasy "Suicidio de uma formiga azul" [The Suicide of the Blue Ant], by the Brazilian Max Carphentier (1945–). Noteworthy in these stories is the specificity of telling detail, akin to Franz Kafka's expressive precision, intended to construct a convincing fantasy realm. Like Kafka's "The Metamorphosis," Sanches's story delves into grotesque and absurd humor; unlike it, "the cripple" does not negate the possibility of transcendence. Sanches treats the existential dilemma of the compulsive personality of his protagonist, a killer of fish, while alluding to the capitalist greed that has proven so destructive of Amazonia's natural integrity. The tragic end of the protagonist seems like poetic justice for an ecological pillager who uses modern technology to obtain greater profit. In contrast to Sanches's narrative, the pieces by Cabral and Carphentier are tender tales of the existential condition, whether the stories are understood literally or as allegories of human predicaments.

Like Sanches, Cabral, and Carphentier, the Bolivian Amazonian author Homero Carvalho (1957–) exhibits a predilection for allegorical or metaphoric stories. Carvalho's story "La Creación" [The Creation] is metaphorically structured by the biblical explanation of the world's genesis. In Carvalho's tale, the creation of a marginal Amazonian rural world goes hand in hand with the degeneration of the region into a traditional Latin American power structure typified by an alliance between the oligarchy and the military, resulting in an exploitative situation often sanctioned—if not altogether facilitated—by the Church.

José Balza is a celebrated fiction writer and essayist born in the Delta of the Orinoco, Venezuela. Evincing an intellectual attitude to literary creation, his works are generally expositions of theory and reflections on the creative process (Berrizbeitia 1990: 75). Balza's aesthetics imply an exploration of language and consciousness that has led him to create metafictions akin to those by the practitioners of the French Nouveau Roman. Balza's story "La sangre" [Blood], for example, has a subtle interplay of subjectivity and outer reality—the implied central theme of the story. His stories and novels are characterized by a luminous linguistic precision. The inclusion of a metafiction such as "La sangre" as part of a regional literature extends the limits of the definition of such literature.

The present selection of Amazonian writing (although not comprehensive because of limitations of space) suggests that rather than speaking of it as a regional writing in its traditional sense we could more justly refer to the creations by Amazonian-born authors as *writing from the region*. The Amazonian region is, in the poetic phrase of Thiago de Mello, "a homeland of the waters" whose literary and cultural territory is in the process of being imagined. Like all projects of identity construction in the present era, that of Pan-Amazonia could appear as a belated and nostalgic Romantic project. Nonetheless, given the emergence of Amazonian cultural consciousness in recent years, such a project is valid. Furthermore, a regional model to study literature, as Amaryll Chanady notes referring to a notion of Antonio Cornejo Polar, is just as useful as a national one (Chanady 1994: xxxiv). The compilation and publication of written and transcribed oral literatures of the regions of the Amazon Basin are of fundamental importance to the identity construction of Amazonia.[2] The Amazonian writing we present here is generally a literature in search of greater expressive freedom, one that has adopted contemporary international trends while not abandoning its roots in the region's syncretic literary and cultural traditions.

With notable regional pride, Luis Hernán Ramírez stated: "One can speak of 'Amazonian literature' in the same sense in which one speaks of Peruvian, Chilean, Bolivian, Cuban or other literatures." However, as we have noted above, Amazonia is not a nation; it is a territory made up of several territories. Nonetheless, like a nation, a literary regional *patria* is a cultural artifact, and the identity construction of such a homeland depends (as does the existence of a nation, in Benedict Anderson's concept) on its inhabitants' communion—or, in this case, the communion among Amazonia's literary and cultural figures. That communion has come to pass.

The Amazonian authors included in this volume celebrate their region's nature without and within. The initial telluric themes and motifs of Amazonia's literature are still present, as well as its reference to an imaginary space nourished by Indigenous and mestizo (in Portuguese, *caboco*) lore. As Amazonian writers we share the distressing burden of a tragic colonial past and a forbidding present in which neocolonial abuses (both external and internal) are all too common. It is not surprising, therefore, that Amazonian writers often become spokespersons for social justice. At the same time they feel bonded to the cadences of their region and in their writing strive to evoke its astonishing and marvelous beauty. They also seek to give meaning to their present and, in doing so, give voice to a forsaken land, and to the anonymous masses of disenfranchised inhabitants of Amazonia. Writing at the margins of the Western world, and sometimes even of their national societies, Amazonian writers continue to strive against the void of a pervasive amnesia.

Notes

1. Amazonian literature may be classified into four categories: (1) Indigenous and mestizo oral literature; (2) the writings by the first chroniclers, explorers, and naturalists; (3) the literary creations from the nineteenth and twentieth centuries by outsiders to the region, including foreign authors drawn by the allure of the exotic environment of Amazonia; and (4) the writings by authors native to Amazonia. The first three categories have been widely published and have been the object of scholarly attention, both within Latin America and beyond it. In contrast, the creations by authors native to Amazonia have remained generally unknown. Alerted by the work we have done at CALC in promoting Amazonian literatures, the editors of the forthcoming *Oxford Comparative History of Latin American Literary Cultures* kindly extended an invitation to me to contribute the introduction and an essay to a section of that encyclopedia entitled "Amazonian Cultural Centres."

In the introduction to the first issue of *Amazonian Literary Review* (1998), I noted the importance of studying and integrating Indigenous and mestizo oral texts in the category of Amazonian literature. Their widespread omission from national anthologies of most countries of the Amazonian Basin speaks to the perpetuation of old prejudices. The works' exclusion, I wrote, was based on a cultural bias—that these works were worthy solely of anthropological consideration. Critics, including the Indigenist Peruvian writer Carlos Mariátegui, also disqualified Indigenous oral texts as literary, basing their judgment on a strict definition of literature as *littera*, or letter, that is, as written text (González Vigil 1990: 150). A debate persists as to whether Amazonian petroglyphs and hieroglyphs are genuine systems of writing (Ypiranga Monteiro 1977: 42).

I stated that Indigenous texts are central to Amazonian studies and noted that the phonetic transcription and translation of such works—with all the limitations and distortions that process implies—have been extensively carried out by anthropologists and ethnographers. However, to claim Indigenous oral literature as the only legitimate Amazonian expression would be limited. "It would be equivalent to claim that the oral traditions of the Sioux, the Apache, Pueblo, Black Foot, Iroquois and other North-American tribes are the only true literature of the United States, to the exclusion of English-speaking works by such authors as Hawthorne, Poe, Emerson, Dickinson, Eliot and Faulkner" (Suárez-Araúz 1998: iv).

The oral *caboco* or *mestizo* folk tradition of Amazonia has been extensively collected and translated into several Western languages. In the last decade, Candace Slater, a professor of literature at the University of California at Berkeley, has contributed two remarkable critical books on the interrelationship of folktales and conceptions of the Amazon: *Dance of the Dolphin: Transformation and Disenchantment in the Amazonian Imagination* and *Entangled Edens: Visions of the Amazon*. The latter is a new study of "an Amazonian-centered poetics," by which Slater means "a systematic of words and images that can help us better understand such seemingly unpoetic concerns as deforestation and species preservation" (2002: 8). Basing much of her envisioning of Amazonia on folk narratives, she argues that "encounters among different myths—including that of a timeless land—have helped to shape the Amazon's myriad realities" (2002: 7).

2. In the last decade of the twentieth century, literary anthologies of Bolivia, Colombia, and Peru have included some transcribed Amazonian Indigenous oral texts, usually in translation into Spanish. See *Historia de la poesía colombiana* (1991), *Nueva historia de la literatura boliviana* (vol. 2, 1995) by Adolfo Cáceres Romero, and *Historia de la literatura peruana* (vol. 9, 1996) by César Toro Montalvo.

Bibliography

Benítez-Rojo, Antonio. *La isla que se repite: El Caribe y la perspectiva posmoderna.* Hanover, N.H.: Ediciones del Norte, 1989.

Berrizbeitia, Josefina. *Balza narrador.* Caracas: Ediciones Octubre, 1990.

Cáceres Romero, Adolfo. *Nueva historia de la literatura boliviana.* Vol. 2. La Paz, Bolivia: Editorial Los Amigos del Libro, 1995.

Chanady, Amaryll, ed. *Latin American Identity and Construction of Difference.* Minneapolis: University of Minnesota Press, 1994.

Cornejo Polar, Antonio. "La literatura latinoamericana y sus literaturas regionales y nacionales como totalidades contradictorias." In *Hacia una historia de la literatura latinoamericana.* Ed. Ana Pizarro. Mexico City: El Colegio de México, 1987. 123–36.

Coutinho, Afranio, and José Galante de Sousa, eds. *Enciclopédia de literatura brasileira.* Rio de Janeiro: FAE-Ministerio de Educação, 1990.

Cunha, Euclides da. *Um paraíso perdido: Reunião de ensaios amazônicos.* Petrópolis, Brazil: MEC, 1976.

Gondim, Neide. *A invenção da Amazônia.* São Paulo: Editora Marco Zero, 1994.

González Vigil, Ricardo. *Retablo de autores peruanos.* Lima: Ediciones Arco Iris, 1990.

Graça, Antônio Paulo. Foreword. *Alameda.* By Astrid Cabral. 1963. Reprint, Manaus: Editora Valer, 1998. 11–20.

———. Foreword. *O outro e outros contos.* By Benjamin Sanches. Manaus: Editora Valer, 1998. 13–20.

Harmon, William, and C. Hugh Holman. *A Handbook to Literature.* 8th ed. Upper Saddle River, N.J.: Prentice Hall, 2000.

Harrison, Marguerite Itamar. "Dois Irmãos: A novel by Milton Hatoum." *Amazonian Literary Review* 3 (2001): 133–35.

Historia de la poesía colombiana. Bogotá: Casa de Poesía Silva, 1991.

León de Hazera, Lydia. *La novela de la selva hispanoamericana.* Bogotá: ICC, 1971.

Maligo, Pedro. *Land of Metaphorical Desires: The Representation of Amazonia in Brazilian Literature.* Wor(l)ds of Change, Latin American and Iberian Literature, 21. New York: Peter Lang, 1998.

Meggers, Betty. *Amazonia: Man and Culture in a Counterfeit Paradise.* Chicago: University of Chicago Press, 1971.

Moraes, Pericles. *Os intérpretes da Amazônia.* Rio de Janeiro: Superintendência de Valorização Econômica da Amazônia, 1959.

Nunes, Benedito. Preface. *Não para consolar: Poesia completa.* By Max Martins. Belém: CEJUP, 1992. 17–43.

Paes Loureiro, João de Jesus. *Cultura amazônica: Uma poética do imaginário.* Belém: CEJUP, 1995.

Ramírez, Luis Hernán. "The First Bards of the Amazon." *Amazonian Literary Review* 1 (1998): 110–33.

Roca García, José Luis. "El tema del trópico en la literatura boliviana." *Signo* 7 (1967).

Rodríguez, Mónica. "La cosmovisión amazónica del cuento moderno peruano." Ph.D. diss. University of Kentucky, 2001.

Santiago, Socorro. *Uma poética das águas: A imagem do rio na poesia amazonense contemporánea.* Manaus: Edições Puxirum, 1986.

Slater, Candace. *Dance of the Dolphin: Transformation and Disenchantment in the Amazonian Imagination.* Chicago: University of Chicago Press, 1994.

———. *Entangled Edens: Visions of the Amazon.* Berkeley: University of California Press, 2002.

Souza, Márcio. "Amazonian Expression." *Amazonian Literary Review* 1 (1998): 134–46.

Stern, Irwin, ed. *Dictionary of Brazilian Literature.* New York: Greenwood Press, 1988.

Suárez-Araúz, Nicomedes. *Amnesis: The Art of the Lost Object.* New York: Lascaux Publishers, 1988.

———. "Breve selección de poesía amazónica." *Presencia Literaria* (La Paz, Bolivia), July 23, 1997.

———. "¿Existe una literatura amazónica boliviana?" *Amazónica* (Trinidad, Bolivia), 2000.

———, ed. *Amazonian Literary Review.* Vols. 1, 2, & 3. Northampton, Mass.: Center for Amazonian Literature and Culture, 1998, 1999, 2001.

Toro Montalvo, César. *Historia de la literatura peruana: Literatura amazónica.* Vol. 8. Lima: A.F.A. Editores, 1996.

———. *Historia de la literatura peruana.* Vol. 9. Lima: Editorial San Marcos, 1996.

Torres-Rioseco, Arturo. *Novelistas contemporáneos de América.* Santiago de Chile: Nascimento, 1939.

Walther, Don H. "Brazilian Prose Fiction: The Amazon Region." Ph.D. diss. University of North Carolina at Chapel Hill, 1948.

Ypiranga Monteiro, Mário. *Fatos da literatura amazonense.* Manaus: Universidade do Amazonas, 1976.

———. *Fases da literatura amazonense.* Manaus: Universidade do Amazonas, 1977.

Poetry

Fig. 1. Alcide d'Orbigny. View of a landscape across the San Mateo River, on the road from Cochabamba to Moxos. Drawing in pencil and charcoal. Paris: Pitois-Levrault & P. Bertrand, 1835. Archivo de Moxos y Chiquitos, Bolivia.

Raúl Otero Reiche
Translated by Nicomedes Suárez-Araúz

The Forest

Cities of the jungle.
I admire their palaces of fragile columns.
The vault encrusted with rare precious stones shimmers.
Millions of giants open up their broad herculean
shoulders in a harmonic stance.
A mere signal could tear up their might
at the edges of the pampa.
Their powerful arms stretch out twisting
in dreadful struggles.
All is potentiality and rhythm, voraciousness and satiety.
A birth before our eyes, a death.
The ash of jaguars fertilizes the protoplasm
of flowers never seen before.
Immense boas ingest the golden bird.
Black flies buzz alongside the butterfly
in its crystalline flight.
A thousand tremulous scales of vibrating atoms
throb in the air:
From a putrid skeleton they rise slowly
purified, slight, ethereal, incorporeal,
breaking up in the prism of humid air,
blended into perfumes, breaths, and colors.
They will enliven the seething blood of wild animals
with renewed demented ardor,
surging into new forms,
new emotions,
so that what had been a lily yesterday now became rancor.

Ceaseless transformation of nature,
leading toward a common destiny, an identical torment.
No one has suffered anything, no one has enjoyed anything.
The demands of life and death are fulfilled.
What mighty spirit an artist's astounded eyes discover
in this nimble and resounding monument, at the same time
powerful and coarse, magnificent, gigantic, rising up
before the horizons!

The jungle is an enormous spreading city.
Bubbling in prolific torrential flow, it renews
its multiple existence.
A monotone bubbling of sap in the sun's fiery cauldrons.
A single impulse stirs the tense muscles
of those fantastic multitudes,
aroused by a strange movement.
It is carved, labeled, written about, chiseled,
without a truce, without rest, endlessly.
Glowing lanterns fuse,
blood-curdling storms liquefy
and at the beat of lightning it sketches butterflies.
The spirit of the jungle builds without rest
this green marvel.
Temples of light, palaces of pure air,
contracting sometimes in the bristling fists
of barbaric notions
much as the tree does to draw forth
its beauty from the fertile breast.

Thus, one day it gave birth to the jungle's work, strange,
stately, variegated, with its indecipherable symbol,
labor of ants, shining dreams of glowworms,
large and brutal persistence of muscles and wings.
This monument has the proportions of a mountain.
Its heights are rounded off by arrow-pointed cusps.
Among them, chiseled cornices form
symmetrical slopes.
Bizarre figures, inconceivable faces,
keep harmony moved solely by the air.
All the errant flocks have stopped their flights
at the subtle edge of the cornices.
The shuddering flight of the snake undulating once
and again imprinted its path.
Cicadas and black silk spiders
embroidered intricate details among the folds
of the arborescent whim of the winds.
And in every corner a monster is carved out in hard stone,
in colossal shapes and seemingly immobile.
There is nothing but thunder settled amid the crest of lightning
and the living sculpture that emerges pulsating
from that whole gathering of images: THE EARTH.

RAÚL OTERO REICHE
Translated by Nicomedes Suárez-Araúz

I Will Complain to God . . .

"I will complain to God about all this,"
he said as he felt the iron at his throat,
and his face showed the unchanging look
of a holy and serene resignation.

Neither the crude threat that breaks down
the strongest will, nor the fatal
torture that horrifies the weak ones,
made him waver from his noble task.

Night became inhabited by visions
emerging in black processions
from the lean and hostile forests.

And as the barbarous torture was applied,
the boughs broke up in the wind
like the arms of giant skeletons.

VIOLETA BRANCA
Translated by R. Kelly Washbourne

Initiation

I don't know who that was who came
with his hands bathed in light
to set the fire of emotions
to the pliant vines of my nerves.
I don't know who came
     to throw stones of my joy
in the dormant waters of my stillness . . .
I don't know who that was . . .

But after the vines
     of my tingling nerves
bloomed in a fleshly flower,
and the waters of my stillness

rippled
    with delicate rings,
my life
since has been a never-ending dawn,
full of unbound wings
and rolling hymns.

———————

Violeta Branca
Translated by R. Kelly Washbourne

My Legend

In the shade of a dark plain where stagnant waters lay
white as the sands and the foaming spray
and sadder than a gesture of farewell,
like the shape of a giant Amazonian lily,
    faint with indifference,
    I bloomed . . .

Tupã,[1] one night,
    looked at me with moonlit eyes
    and fell in love.
And with words that recalled the smooth
    laughter of the waters
running over stones, said:

"You are beautiful and sad. Thus
    you shall have the highest glory,
which is greater than the triumphal poem
the *virapura*[2] sings in its clear, clear voice.
Take the *muiraquitã*[3] stone,
go down to the depths of the waters:
you will be Yara."[4]

Then . . .
in a moment of enchantment and beauty,
with my hair wrapped in aquatic plants
and in my body the spell of mysteries,
I caught the naïve soul of a careless sailor.
And the legendary god of Amazonia,
feeling love throb in my song,
    spoke again to me.

On that day his eyes
    shone like sunbeams
and his voice resounded like the roaring tidal bore:

"You no longer are worthy of the glory of being Yara,
you shall not remain here even a single day.
You will receive your punishment . . ."

And he turned me into a woman.

1. In Tupy lore, the supreme Indigenous deity responsible for separating sun and moon, god of good who presides over all human affairs.—Ed.

2. Uirapuru [Virapura] is a talismanic bird of legend whose beautiful song attracts other birds.—Ed.

3. From the Nhamundá River, the muiraquitã is a rare green stone the Amazon women of legend gave their lovers as talismans after three days and nights of love.—Ed.

4. The "Mother of the Waters," Yara, or Iara, in mythology is said to be a siren who attracts *caboclos* with her song and drags them to the depths of the river at Turanã, outside Manaus.—Ed.

VIOLETA BRANCA
Translated by R. Kelly Washbourne

Nightfall

Like a great bloodied bird wounded,
the dusk falls heavy and sanguine
over the welcoming silence of this verandah.
The shadows meekly envelop objects,
while bitterly I sense that other shadows,
heavier and darker, are layering my affections
with tedium and disillusion.
I look out on the sea, thick with the fury of the plea,
with the wind strong and the rocks steep.
In the skies, the blaze of colors waning . . .
It is the night on the waters, in me and on the verandah
where alone, I am remembering loves
and having more discreet dreams and desires.
I feel strange amid things so beloved,
lost in the shadows that envelop objects
and—pained—I see the dark form looming
that enfolds and wrecks the things I love.

JULIO DE LA VEGA
Translated by Alice R. Clemente

The Legend of "El Dorado" and the Reality of "El Gran Paitití"[1]

The legend took its first steps
when it called out "El Dorado"
sounding like a gong in the distance,
and over the ancient continent
spread his voices . . .

Through plazas with street lamps
and wind in intricate alleys
the legend rolled:
"Out there in the eye of the jungle,
where the world ends,
behind the cinnamon
there is a ruling god of fire,
with gold rings in his ears
and on his head luminous bands,
his rings
are of the richest metal
and he is the lord of the jungle's thunder."

And in the sleepy streets,
next to the doors of churches,
in manor houses and castles
adventurous horsemen
told themselves, as one tells of a kiss,
that out there in the eye of the jungle
the valiant will be rich . . .

. . . After nights with lightning,
downpours in the rigging
and hurricanes in their sails
new seas appeared
in the pupils of the watchmen . . .
During long shoreless nights
they climbed the waves
and crossed green waters.
Over the waves, sharks;

and beneath the sky, the gulls.
And the anchor clawed the beaches
beside the Cross and swords . . .

1. Local name for "El Dorado" in the region of Moxos, eastern Bolivia.—Ed.

JULIO DE LA VEGA
Translated by Alice R. Clemente

The Conquistadors in the Jungle

They touched the lung of the mountain,
they saw the condor light on their shoulders
and caressed the puma's hip,
they saw spiders on their helmets
and wore snakes like shawls . . .
In the clearings in the green
they pitched their tents
and the bivouac of anguish burned.
Tigers and panthers leapt
near a howl of green eyes . . .
In an aurora of toucans
the fever of armor dawned . . .
Over the pastures of dew they rode out new routes
opening streets in the jungle,
they fell along the roads with a murmur of dry leaves . . .

But in the eye of the jungle
"El Gran Paitití" called with his gong . . .
A thousand times the tapirs trod them
but the blades of lances
pierced wild boars . . .

In boats of the jungle's wood
the men swept the rivers . . .
Then from new gulfs
they traveled up the waters
and past the curve of islands
navigated their anxieties . . .

Like the silence of churches,
solemn, dark like a temple
was the hidden path . . .

Over the thirst of coarse lips,
with spines in their backs
and bare feet
they went on lifting their pain
down the path of hope . . .

But man is blinded amid false splendors . . .
and "El Gran Paitití" spoke:
"The land is the contentment of men,
here,
from this wood, cabins will rise,
under these shadows and over these pastures
the men of tomorrow will spring forth . . ."

The men of Iberia never understood the message,
they offered their throats to the fangs
and gave their veins to be filled
with the poison of vipers,
because in the eye of the jungle
the gong of "Paitití"
was but a human voice and a message:
"The land alone is the wealth!"

MAX MARTINS
Translated by R. Kelly Washbourne

Erasures

> A bottomless hole full of words
> *Hakuin*

My name is a river
My name is a river that lost its name

                              A river

neither yes
nor no

Where
         Paltry stream
         Water masturbated in shoals
                  deep pools
      pool-
              looted climax through varicose veins
        Semen same man
             sans me
Where is my name Out There in this amnesiac, wayward river
                of mud?
On the bloated fault of this crumpled bed?
My name is an amputated stump of a river—an Icon
              Of baroque
                  clay
A river that only says itself
        Beds itself
              trokes and soaks
and sinks in ego as he goes : Aquarius
My name is a stopped-up river
         (well)
        And here my name broke
           off its journey and bone
Is this where it cracked? And is its face this
           darkness
behind the door
        mirror
exposed to fever
        to the beast within?
           Self-absorbed,
my name is a river that has no cure

———————

MAX MARTINS
Translated by R. Kelly Washbourne

Meditation for Bashô
For Age de Carvalho

Stone
Penetrates the silence

Solitary stone-silence

The cricket penetrates the silence The voice
The solitary voice The stone The temple The cricket
The temple The cricket penetrates the silence: The solitary voice

The solitary voice The stone The temple the cricket penetrates
The cricket penetrates the silence: The solitary voice
Solitary stone: The temple The cricket
penetrates the silence: The voice

Stone-temple
Silence

———————

Max Martins
Translated by R. Kelly Washbourne

Final Cycle

These roots in one hand
like gnarled, frightened
serpents,
bleed.

And in the other, severed,
the tendon rests separate
from the skein.

Between the two, the sword of the Gospel,
the flies, the stones, the innards.
And between the legs the solitary beast
howls at the far-off waning moon.

And here you are, on bended knee,
Your breast smoldering
And your tongue in flames.

MAX MARTINS
Translated by R. Kelly Washbourne

The Thing

On the other side of the gaze
the lunar cupola that weaves
sphere and gauze
the sleepless thing
of sweat and incense
gasping breathless bent
more than fruit
or petal or war
almost dying
submerged is born
in time and passion
mass
sour spit: the noun

MAX MARTINS
Translated by R. Kelly Washbourne

Max, Skinny Poet

Max, skinny poet
in the calm of the water-color meadows
by chance did you love the lily
plucked in haste
between your shoes?
Could you have found
instead of the flower
the knife-blade
inside the flower?

Look in your pocket for the compass
and the anchor in your chest
from this ship in your throat,
ready to set sail.
On the rusty keel,
on the shriveled prow

You will discover the island
Meager poet, you still take note
of the sun on the walls
but what of the salt
that courses through the stones?

At the unexpected stillness of a wing
behold the fly:
in his belly seethes the poem.

Thiago de Mello
Translated by R. Kelly Washbourne

Son of the Jungle . . .

Son of the jungle, water and wood
come in the light of my eyes,
and explain this way I have of loving stars
and of bearing this cross of hope.
An unkind cut disgraces the wood,
the powerful water of childhood arrives, cleanses.
I came of age amid the wood,
the soaked logs, unseasoned wood,
my mother complained of the smoke.
I actually opened my eyes and saw wood,
the beautiful laurel woodwork
in my grandfather's house in Bom Socorro,
where my father was born
and where I was born as well.

I was the last to see the house still standing,
its intact joists were bowed,
a dwelling for bats and termites.
Until it was pulled down by the currents of many high waters,
the house was swamped
in a silence made of slime and leaves and tiles.

But the house did not die for good
when the beams of memory tumbled down
                              in my father's mind,
in this, the summer of his ninetieth year.

For more than half a century,
without returning to the place where he was born,
the house still stood in his memory,
the windows open to the mornings
of Paraná do Ramos,
the fiddlewood staircase
that he would still go down
to tread the dewy grass
and to walk, almost running,
through the common fields covered in silk-cotton trees
all the way to the flowered banks of Lago Grande
where adolescent hands learned
the secrets of cow udders.

Wherever he went, my father took along the house
and the hammock stretched between *acariquara* trees,
where, cradled in the mosquito silence,
he and my mother embraced,
cloaked by an overpowering sky
full of stars.

One night, the two of us alone,
in a silence now almost impossible
in the present-day frazzle of Manaus,
my father asked me if I remembered
a jungle sound that he heard
in the clear early morning, his arrival
from Bom Socorro burning in his memory
after much rowing and so many waters.
I said nothing. I kept listening
to my father making his way amid the mango trees
toward that thud, that
dry, steely thud, that singing
steel on wood—it was your mother,
her hair flowing in the sun, it was Maria,
brandishing her ax and splitting
blue mulatto wood, as hard as bronze, into logs;
buffeted by the wind, she stood alone
in the middle of the jungle.
All those things resurfaced
and suddenly came together in his memory,
while the tumbledown house was given

to ravenous abandonment, prickly-weed,
and the old forsaken cacao grove
yielded its fruit to the cries of monkeys
and parrots reveling in the sun.

Meanwhile my lonesome grandmother Safira,
the house's last true inhabitant,
would wake in the dawn to wait
for a canoe that would never return.
Safira, the rock of the waters,
gave me her blessing like
one who drops the hook to pull out
a *jaraqui* fish into the *paronga* gourd.
Always dressed in black,
her gravelly voice hid
the tenderness of stars
at dawn over the Andirá.[1]

Son of the jungle, water, and wood,
I returned to help build
our future home. Race of pith,
one day the luminous prows will come
to free all green from slavery.

1. River southwest of Parantins.—Trans.

THIAGO DE MELLO
Translated by R. Kelly Washbourne

Bearings
To Geir Campos

I only am in verse.
My most diverse personae
are ancient labyrinths
that confound and lose me.

My thought bores
through walls of nothingness, in search
of what I never was nor will be.

Around pale female flesh

my body resurrects
to volunteer what I am not.

My walk, my gestures
ill proclaim, if at all they do,
my yet-unshaken permanence.

To get to where
I do not try to be, but *am,*
I go on shaped like a word.

————————

THIAGO DE MELLO
Translated by R. Kelly Washbourne

I Fear for My Eyes

I fear for my eyes
faced with honorable vestments.
Meanwhile, I have my wants.

Fear that suggests the aftermath
to being a broken pitcher
at the prodigal well.

To not observing, I prefer
total blindness.

Not like blind men,
but like the feet of children,
which as they walk are blind.

————————

THIAGO DE MELLO
Translated by Charles Cutler

In Confidence

All in all I was a small winner
in a century out of control:
the one that's leaving now, leaving love
to death's toll.

I came away with flowers. The secret
of so many, I once knew.
Among the blessings I have scars
of the pain that was my due.

From only one thing I take solace:
I lived life wholly.
With me ends the sadness
of losing what I loved.

Defrontre do Ramos, 1998.

THIAGO DE MELLO
Translated by Charles Cutler

Fleeting Miracle

For the song of Nilson Chaves

I'm always in awe when
my body proves worthy of you.
With all its limits and flaws
(the river still flows through me),
I swell and marvel
at the sorcery of the gift.

Skin becomes dew,
hair turns to forest,
pure sweetness the fire,
a revelry of sighs.

Like a child,
eyes radiant,
held spellbound
by his magic kite
dancing in the sky, I'm astounded
before the soft glow
of your star-filled face
and I record in my heart the songs
of rapt birds
rising from your lips.

After Easter Island,
Spring 1994.

Thiago de Mello
Translated by Charles Cutler

My Own Death

Death belongs to me. I mean, my death.
The one I was born with. She lives in me,
off me. She depends on what I am
and what I do. The things she does with me,
she doesn't mean any harm and she has every right
to divide up her life with mine.
Death, she doesn't wish me any harm. She's fine
with the laws of my being, with secrets
she knows maybe better than I do.

She welcomes the warm place in my body
where she was born and where every day
she takes a little bit more, but never in a greedy way.

It's only me death is leading on. She doesn't mean any
harm. She could even be my friend.
It's true that I've made it easy for her from time to time.
It's not for nothing that I'm her favorite meal.
I don't want to harm her either. My friend!
It's the right thing to tell her now. Once my life's
over, all the miracles and the mystery,
a life she always took advantage of,
death, my death, will die along with me.

The two of us, now one, what will be next?
The Beyond doesn't faze me. I'll settle for the here-and-now.

Parintins, Itatiba, 1998.

Luiz Bacellar
Translated by Alexis Levitin

Sonnet of the Pencil

I've raised you as a mast of black
from which to rig my sail of love,

oh cylinder of pine above
your straight and strictly governed track.

Thanks for your lines so cruel and clean,
my deeply rooted graphite core,
now comes along a bright machine
to duplicate you, what a bore,

to multiply your evil deed
of fixing on that blank white space
the fleeting sounds I softly glean.

Why does this carbon pistil need
to fossilize, without a trace
of life, light flowers of a dream?

LUIZ BACELLAR
Translated by Alexis Levitin

Rondel of the Mango

odorous mango
roseate golden
they call you rose
they call you rapier
part rapier part rose
artfully composed
in the amorous mold
of a heart

from your foliage flow
dark shadows below
and roots along the road
while your bark declares
barred with old scars
a hardened cold despair

Luiz Bacellar
Translated by Alexis Levitin

Rondel of the Banana

where does a banana
sweet chrysalis
sleep? in the green
hammock of its skin
hidden within
so gentle so harmless
so very pachydermous
reclusive this muse is

a white shape sways
all ways and all days
and dreams in the breeze
of its own sweet ease
divine spirit
outlined in purity

Luiz Bacellar
Translated by Nicomedes Suárez-Araúz

Haiku

The root distills
the soil and falls:
open fruit.

Lightning flashes.
Thunderclap, wind, drizzle.
Moon rising.

Lost in the grass
the cricket answers back
to the bird's song.

Scissor tails,
swallows slice the air:
season of the moths.

A dragonfly invades
the living-room where three poets
talk about the spring.

Spring light
in the flowing mist:
bamboo leaf.

The full moon rises
the provider fills up
the bowl with rice.

A cracked plate?
No, a dry branch
before the full moon.

In the midst of the dry
grass of the field
the sunflower stands fast.

The scarab rolls up
in a little ball of dung
future time.

Will the leaves cover
the silver box
I lost in the jungle?

New York

The blind street musician
sets down an old mug
collects a snowflake.

Jorge Tufic
Translated by R. Kelly Washbourne

Jurupari[1]

Before descending to earth,
Tupã, the thunder-god, called Jurupari
and said to him: Here are

the seeds of the animals,
and the still-small body
of laws that will protect
the truth that will be
your kingdom, against the
lust for gold and clammy skin
of those who are coming from the sea
into the river mouth.

1. God or cultural figure of several Amazonian tribes.—Ed.

Jorge Tufic
Translated by Erik L. Iana

Kites

Puppets in the blue
on invisible string
—their gestures slide
on the scales of the wind.

At the silken blows
the warm blood
of the summer bursts, breaking
on the crests of dreams.

They are crafty lessons
of fragility; and how
with sticks and paper
one builds a poem.

Jorge Tufic
Translated by Erik L. Iana

The Egg

the space of the song
is the space of the bird;
the down quivers within
the opening of the womb.

the space of the song
is the eye inside
of the open spaces
that create the bird.

the space of the song
opens up in the time
that heralds the bird:
it breaks itself free.

JORGE TUFIC
Translated by Charles Cutler

Haiku

(The Four Seasons)
Just the leaf and frog.
The air giddily seeds
the new day.

Raucous thunder
couples with the cicada
and makes the summer

(Art Nouveau)
In the old cornice
of a building tedium stirs,
an angel pees.

Ah, such grace:
the fly, uncouth grand dame,
dances on the table.

An island tremulous
in the mirror of water. Red
the saber of the moon.

In the clinch of the profligate vine
the stalwart sandalwood:
dribbling, sucking death.

When it grows dark
the glowworm lights its fire
there at the foot of the wall.

Petals of myself
I grow in an old pitcher.
Once it was a garden.

———————

GERMÁN LEQUERICA PEREA
Translated by Frederick H. Fornoff

From "Arms Crossed"

Waiting
arms crossed
man always destroys the word

If you could say whatever the cost
—man sleeping
child taking giant steps on the sidewalk
woman sad and hurting
washerwoman of stars and breezes—
how many times I've seen you on your knees

If only you could say
as I say
—no excuse for the times I was drunk—
how much your eyes, your shoulders hurt
how much you have to pay for this bread they give you
so grudgingly

If you could see my children running wild
in precise time
with my ordained sorrows
If you could see those tiny
tiny feet
wasting a whole year
in the month of each day
such innocence

In short
if you could just

get past your arms
past everyone's flagrant arms
to hold him high in the middle of the street

If you could go with me
to meet night's rebel voices
together in the heat of rifles
in the song of the wind
in the jungle
we'd be able to tell those who suffer
that it won't be long till each ripple in the river
sings out its joyous descent to the sea
once and for all
as if its joy were love's own cornstalk

GERMÁN LEQUERICA PEREA
Translated by Frederick H. Fornoff

From "The Quest for Dawn"

The quest for dawn in this valley
where man is an indefinable substance
where you can feel the opium
constricting the throat of the villages
and where coldness
the abyss
even the desolation of the workers
their bitter bread
is a bottomless glass day after day

The quest for dawn
—I repeat—
is a lofty minute
a pain with thorns like a huge birth
a sea of stumbles

It's a warm embrace from afar
a fierce cell
an exile of feathers in mid-flight
a trapped bird's genuine bitterness

But also
brother
the first nation of our fight
the true direction of the wind
the very first flag of our rifles

———————

GERMÁN LEQUERICA PEREA
Translated by Frederick H. Fornoff

From "Suspended in Air"

And that's why I protest
never breaking
It's why I try
to awaken the shadow
the hesitant gaze
the precise contrition annihilates it

And that's why
I protest
sad as can be
about the Andes moaning
to dance the *huayno*[1]
dreaming of the knotted *quipus*[2]
For the sake of the spirit that burnishes the bees
at the break of every dawn
sad about man so long oppressed
by the dead letter of hymns

It's why I want to stop the farce
to find someone to live with
to shame time
to divide the word into its proper syllables
It's why I keep fighting
battling the wind
impregnating every roadside inn with my heat
swimming blithely
across the jungle's
temporal rivers

1. A social dance dating from the time of the Incas. It is a scarf dance accompanied by *sicuri* bands or by harp, guitars, bass drum, and charango (10-string lute) combos.—Ed.

2. Inca system of record keeping and communication through a code of knotted strings.—Ed.

JACQUELINE DE WEEVER

Creations

When the gods arrive
cassava dough shatters.

Poison extracted, ground,
kneaded with knotted muscle

dough shatters, combines anew,
perhaps the same but different.

The gods arrive. Sulphur butterflies
beat wings to chase cells into storms

catastrophe derived from gossamer wings,
small wonders wander, wrapped in silence.

Knives rattle when the gods arrive,
ready to carve flute from bone.

JACQUELINE DE WEEVER

Moon Dancing

The black crow's
caws welcome
the rising moon
as it traces
the circle of an hour's dance.

His black shadow
dances in the milk
from the moon-jug
as it washes
the terrace, a belt of white.

His harsh caw
stops in mid-throat,
lassoed by the moon
as its sashes
spring across the sky.

The black crow
partners and squires
the moon in slow moves
as it tangos
toward the new year.

———————

ALCIDES WERK
Translated by José M. Rodeiro

The Lake of 7 Islands

On the Lake of 7 Islands
there are 7 islands planted
and a green world surrounds them.

On each island there is a stilt-house
in each house a lovely virgin
in each pure girl a love.

In the Lake of 7 Islands
there are fishes, there are turtles
and the bewitching river dolphin.

From the dark soil of the lake
a thousand Amazonian lilies grow
in each, a glorious flower.

On the Lake of 7 Islands
keeper of the enchanted gift
of being the Equator's native son,

there are 7 lovely women
living in stilt-houses
each of them dreaming of her lover.

On the Lake of 7 Islands
counting all the maiden daughters
of the *caboclo* fisherman

there are 7 expectant mothers
for having loved the landscape so
and the philandering dolphin.

———————

ALCIDES WERK
Translated by José M. Rodeiro

The Meeting of the Waters

> If you and I were these two rivers, Maria,
> every time we came upon each other,
> what Amazon river of love would not flow
> from me, from you, from us so deeply in love.
> *Quintino Cunha*

Negro and Solimões[1]
—two titans battling,
astonished by their sudden encounter.
Later, in a friendly embrace,
in peace,
two mighty forces become one.
And together they go on to tell
the Atlantic their adventures.

1. The rivers Negro and Solimões (another name for a stretch of the Amazon River) merge their tannin dark and white silt waters upstream from Manaus. The spectacle they produce is a popular tourist attraction.—Ed.

———————

ALCIDES WERK
Translated by José M. Rodeiro

The River's Night

On this night beyond compare,
soaked in shadows
I ran away from home, ran away
to the luminous whiteness of this beach,

as if the dawn I seek
had drowned in this river.

I must wake up the river,
who is exhausted from all his travels,
hoping to find relief
from the death I carry in me
full of tales of gigantic snakes
and of fishermen long dead,
part of this river
and just the same as me.

In a sky full of clouds
there are clouds filled with rain:
why then does it not rain? I want
to be drenched by this night,
to tremble with hunger and cold
to purify my ills
to leave my body empty
guarding this useless castle
and set out to search the dawn
so it arrives in haste
to bathe the river's waters,
so my face may be scarred
by the winds with which I struggled.

———————

ALCIDES WERK
Translated by José M. Rodeiro

The Green

There's a dream in your soul,
That fulfills its role
with life.

There's a magic power in your hands
that knows life's bountifulness,
and sets down its roots.

There's a miracle in your love,
that bears flowers and fruits
and perpetuates itself.

There can be no success
for the builders of deserts
and hunger,
as long as we can repeat,
in each generation,
the simple gestures of your clean hands
and of your word,
for the love of the green.

ASTRID CABRAL
Translated by Alexis Levitin

Ritual

Every evening
I water the plants around the house.
And beg the trees to pardon me
this paper where I plant these
words of stone,
watered as I weep.

ASTRID CABRAL
Translated by Alexis Levitin

Porto Seguro 1980

For Kátia Bento

Bead necklaces and feathers still
but the air and the sea
no longer those
of full-sailed caravels
conquering dead calms.
Nor are the lands those
of Caminha's[1] letters home.
There is oil on the waves
and rare the birds
that fly through thinning forests
sown with smoldering charcoal pits.

Rare those parrots
with rainbows in their wings.
Rare those fish
in nets of freshest dawn.
Survivors, the Pataxós [2]
living victims
of our greedy ancestors,
corsairs like no others,
divvying up this new world
in Tordesillas [3] slices
gulping down lands and rivers
blood gushing forth in battles
cannons against arrows.
Today to keep tradition going
we buy touristic cudgels
and bows as well to decorate
our bourgeois walls.
For some Caiambá's [4] paltry
copper coins we snatch from them
those last remaining feathers
that no longer cover their
ancient splendid nakedness,
their bodies somber now,
clothed in misery.
And so I wrap myself in painful plumes
but not of birds:
rather those of late-arriving vain remorse
in which I atavistic dress
in this fragmenting hour of the wreck.

1. Pero Vaz de Caminha: sixteenth-century chronicler of voyages.—Trans.
2. Decimated Amazonian tribe.—Trans.
3. Treaty of 1494 dividing South America between the Spanish and the Portuguese.—Trans.
4. Another much-reduced Amazonian tribe.—Trans.

Astrid Cabral
Translated by Alexis Levitin

Everywhere the River

Everywhere the river
serpent at large crawling
across a countryside of open plains
tamed snake broken by
banks and manacles of bridges
or captive fragment in a jug
in the concave palm of a dipping cup
in a translucent little mug
milk swelling a gourd's breast.
In baptismal waters I take communion
and submerge this ancient body
of a shadowy amphibian past,
all of us so saurian,
so close to fish and turtle,
and I mirror the fleeing face
through waters equally fugitive
and with me goes the river gliding
grinding grinning gripping rivering underme,
in an underworld of dreams.

Astrid Cabral
Translated by Alexis Levitin

River Dolphin in the Body

It flows in the depths of the body, a dark river
of muddied waters and deep desires
ancestral lymph midst furriness and urgency.
In it dwells a river dolphin, ready for the leap,
and it attacks so other rivers may be spawned
and life may not abort, but gush, gush forth forever.

Elson Farias
Translated by Jean R. Longland

The Medicine Man

Whenever the smoke was rising
behind the belt of green,
Catingueira was at home.
From all the rivers came
the sick in soul and body,
more in soul than in body,
since the body is a tributary
of the soul as the smaller rivers
are tributaries of the greater.
Men with cuts and slashes,
girls bitten by fishes,
sorrowful barren women,
all came. Catingueira
was the beginning of life
or else the force that sustains
life, beginning and end.
His word was sufficient,
and his hypnotic gaze,
his presence, merely his presence,
for everything to be cured.
What his eyes did not see,
or lips and tongue feel,
were teas of garden leaves,
bark of bitter trees,
ointments of Pau Santo,[1]
purest mother's milk.
—Catingueira's plasters,
wanting all fame to flee
for wealth is not his goal.
Beings from the sloping shores
that storms transfigure
or figure in those men
possessed of god or demon,
and vibrate as the root
vibrates along the banks,
give health to him who sickens,
make the unhappy happy.

When Catingueira would go
to heal in the patient's house,
he did not row, he sat
like the river king on the bench
under the canoe canopy.
Little land he possessed
in the areas of nothingness,
his only domain consisted
of unreal real estate:
much planting and tending of myths,
acres of gross abuses
and the living legend sprouting
along the straight-flowing rivers.
Catingueira in his house
was the thin white thread of smoke
rising behind the jungle,
—a strip that the river covers,
the houses of small estates
and the hovels of the poor.

1. Pau Santo, literally "holy wood," is an Amazonian tree that harbors deadly red
ants.—Ed.

ELSON FARIAS
Translated by Jean R. Longland

Rain Patterns

1
The living leaves
living resins
wispy insects
mimosa droplets.

As you suffered
incipient stem
torso of roses
bluish breasts.

Drenched in rain
the greater pain
of gentle mist,

liquid plume
play of spume
of green pain.

2
The rain passes.
Green clay pitcher
fish that gnaw
the chrome. Carnations:

you were on earth
crude clay
edge of lake waters
dung of oxen.

Silent fingers
fashioned you into
exact form.

Today you are a vase
freely resting
on this balcony.

3
Little girls
leaving the bath
naked in the valley
of the yielding earth.

In the rain the plants
crisscross coldly
stinging nettles
velvety roses.

Their branches weave
sheets of sorrows
for the mornings

calm young girls
innocent of heartbreak
lively and well.

ELSON FARIAS
Translated by Alice R. Clemente

From A Ballad Book of Creation

They cut out a place for the village
occupied with that
by order of their grandmother.
—You are two and you must build
a village.
They cut down trees
while their sex spoke:
—A sex for Mawarye!
—What is he saying, Woxke?[1]
—Go see.
And they cut the trees they felled.
But there was no sound of sex
and Mawarye cut again,
—A sex for Mawarye!
—Go see, Woxke.
and he found the sex moving
from one place to another
and called out again:
—Mawarye, Mawarye, come now.
—Very well, very well.
Woxke looked around in surprise:
—What is this?
—It looks like it is our sex.
And they snatched it up from the ground
and put it on.

1. Mawarye and Woxke are Indigenous astral beings that perpetually relive the birth of sexual consciousness and pleasure.—Ed.

João de Jesus Paes Loureiro
Translated by Charles Cutler

Psalm XIV

Behold the way of the Cycle.

The lament begins again,
my lament of Achilles
Indian-Amazonia slain in her own beauty.

The carcass of the fish on the rocks,
under banners of ruin,
altar in flames
thick bundle of myths
left by its side,
prisoner of my own skin.

The biblical beetle,
vestal virgin on steady wing,
                              falls upon

the victim
            stirs
            stirs and begins to dance
            —ships burn all around

Behold the way of the Cycle
Gone forever the river's body
                              never touching shore
            waist
                              body of green
            neck
                                          tattoos . . .
            veins

            In the forest
                        in the havens
            at the crossings
                        in rivulets
            beneath angels of stone and godless staffs,
            shadowy priestesses lead the ceremony . . .

JOÃO DE JESUS PAES LOUREIRO
Translated by Charles Cutler

Idyll De-Myth I

Quivering sleep
shifts on mats of silent strings.
The theater of drums,
    rich song of flutes,
    rhythms from distant hollows.
And bulldozers burst forth against the myths.

Celestial birds, Indians, squatters
profaned in the tangle of the world.
Canoes drift off course.

May 1976
In Parcel 17 death runs rampant
Hellfire of cattlemen and landowners
and on the altars of law,
pianissimo, squatters feed the flames.
The lamb of God among the parrots,
always to blame,
    like the stray dog.
(Love's sails in shreds,
rudders broken apart,
the heart, out of its body,
in pieces . . .)

Death occupies
the guard of Parcel 17 and his wife.
It wasn't the doings of Big Snake or the Evil Eye,
it wasn't Wicked Witch, Malaria Monster, Evil Omen,
it wasn't the Forest Queen, Black Magic,
or the Screech Bird[1] either. This one was
Death Imported, real death,
death in ambush, remorseless death,
Death on the books, all tallied up, debts cleared,
death that is one's final loss,
for it turns into land,
and that land belongs
to someone else . . .

1. Legendary figures that the Amazonian popular imagination attributed to ill omens.—Ed.

———————

João de Jesus Paes Loureiro
Translated by Charles Cutler

Bar Do Parque[1]

Tubercular night coughs up morning.
The adolescent
              —mask of the gods—
moved among silent tables
with gigantic crustacean claws
bleeding the unmoved faces
of those
          whose hands
                 under tables
were engaged in clandestine games.
Couples dreaming with the promise of lovemaking
in webs of hammocks among mango trees.
       Vultures confabulate with bats
                in dark spaces between lights.

Two women looking at each other for centuries
    wait for a miracle.

Someone under the underpass masturbates to
         Gregorian chants
         soaring up from the footlights
         at the Teatro da Paz.
Sweat and sperm soak the ballerina
         choreographically making love between scenes.

           Violence is making its rounds in the deep of night.
Mouths like shells
           cultivate pearls, kisses.

The tables are full.
         Many are drinking
their daily dose of low spirits.

1. Built in 1898 as the ticket booth of the Teatro da Paz. At the beginning of the twentieth century, it became a kiosk bar where the political and intellectual elite of Belém do Pará gathered.—Ed.

João de Jesus Paes Loureiro
Translated by Charles Cutler

Workers

In the background
                ancient silhouettes of churches.
Close by,
hale mango trees
nodding with green fruit
to the song of *sabiá* and canary
                      velvet voices
perched eternal on silent branches.

But the factory horn blares,
                despair dressed in smoke.
Disposable parts, workers, shut down machines.
Sit at the curb.
Open tin-foil lunches.
Eat cold beans, cold rice, cold egg.
Empty, the body's sanctuary of food and love.
Forks, knives, spoons are now just tools.
Mechanically tightening up things, turning screws against hunger.
Chewing of gears
jaws, bunches of springs,
oiled by saliva.

They sit at the curb
                with the factory straight across,
they always seem to be sideways.
Off to the side,
           like things
we don't have the guts to face.

FERNANDO URBINA RANGEL
Translated by Frederick H. Fornoff

Genesis

The Mother was there,
potency of seeds hidden
in the dark womb of silence.

And then came the vibration . . .
A word started to emerge from the fertile abyss.
The winged Being initiated its flight, generating upwardness.
Wings spread,
it covered the shadow of downwardness
in the vast copulation.

Afterwards, the Son would come,
heir to all the words,
the ones that on a distant dawn
would be rock and river for knowing time,
fields and groves
for naming the bird and the wind,
and flesh of beast,
and man,
the one lurking in the night, fashioning nostalgia.

Bogotá, September 8, 1994

Based on Abyayalensan traditions. The Tule Indians (Kunas) gave the name Abya Yala to the continent that was later named America, most arbitrarily. The expression means "Tierra en plena madurez" [Earth ripe and complete], a meaning that contradicts the term *Nuevo Mundo* [New World], which denotes something yet to be fulfilled, something unfinished.—Author

---

FERNANDO URBINA RANGEL
Translated by Frederick H. Fornoff

The Arrow

Behind me my arrows
rattle in their quiver.

Six arrows, I carry six arrows.

One is for the stag
who is flight in infancy
when his hoof
barely grazes the plain.

Another for cutting short
that other flight of blue doves
at dusk.

The third that will gem-fix
the dazzle of the fish
in the crystals of the pool.

Each arrow has its own name.
Serpent-arrow, hiding its slim death
in the grass;
jaguar-arrow,
poised claw that makes us
a shiver lying in wait.

Arrow of black feathers,
the one I saved for Man.

He too carries his arrows,
and my name is on one.

Bogotá, May 10, 1981

FERNANDO URBINA RANGEL
Translated by Frederick H. Fornoff

Echo

The Father was seated in the Silence
ripening silences.

Thunder hadn't been invented,
or the rustling of wind through leaves,
or the roar of the jaguar, or the shriek of eagles,
or the thorn-voice of the mosquito.

With whom can the god speak?

Then he saw his shadow.
It was there, seated.
The word was invented, and echo responded
(echo is the shadow of sound).

Now I have a companion,
said the Father.
In this way men were formed.
That's why we sit with the Father
and when he lifts his voice in the rite
we repeat his last words.

Bogotá, April 1995
Based on a myth narrated by the grandfather Chuumu Güio of the Muinane Nation.—
Author

César Calvo
Translated by Nicomedes Suárez-Araúz

Amazon

Thousands of moons ago
when the world was shadow,
before God was born,
when the world was shadow,
a lightning bolt struck a rosewood tree
from heaven.

A lightning bolt struck a rosewood tree
from heaven
and its branches sprung up
a most beautiful woman,
it happened thousands of years ago
when the world was shadow.

For a long, long time
that beautiful woman,
the child of lightning
and a rosewood tree,
ran through the forests,
naked, sad and lonely.

And she cried so much, so much,
our first love,
and cried, and cried
longing to be a wife,
that from her ceaseless weeping
the Amazon began.

Afterwards, no one heard
from that beautiful woman again.
All that is known
is that the world was shadow
and that lightning struck
a rosewood tree.

———————

César Calvo
Translated by Nicomedes Suárez-Araúz

Untitled

> Conspire with the statues
> for they
> won't betray you.
> *Germán Lequerica Perea*

Last night, going down the street in my dream, a raging mob, armed
with sticks and scorn, pursued a man because instead of a body he had a
mirror. It was a dead-end street, as narrow as an alley, and sharp, and
paved with skulls, and foreheads of skulls he stepped on, he skipped,
struggling, bones of gray souls, and he flew on, leaving no trace, bleached
souls. And at the end of the dead-end street, I remember it well, there
was a tiny door which he could pass only by crouching down and that
small door led to another dead-end street and so on, to the infinite. And
the infinite was there, in my dream, carpeted with skulls. And just as the
mob was about to grab him, I woke up. Startled, on my pillow I caught
by surprise the texture and gleam of a mirror. Yes: that little mirror
through which my mother saw my age behind her eyes. I thought she
had placed it there on purpose, at my headboard, so that I would see how
I take my time in getting up. Tormented, I seized the mirror and dashed
it against the floor. But, from the shards of that looking-glass moon, the
same raging mob turned against me. And I've had to fall asleep once
more.

César Calvo
Translated by Laura A. Kennedy

Untitled

Blown from its pedestal by a single breath, my forehead
among blades of glass, nonetheless,
oppressed by the invincible weight of absence, guides
the course of the stars and their suicidal brightness.

Instead of knocking it down, I love my statue.
At the base of its ashes, growing old, I lie down.

I love this senseless library,
this mouth of bone,
my voice, my void, and its blind horse.

César Calvo
Translated by Grace Rugg

Untitled

Reveal, in your finery, not just cornices but
dizziness where the sleeping infants stagger
and wake the elderly who are already far
from shore
and hugging the body of a log for dear life!

You'll be able to read in deep stars
or perennial ones
and you won't want to believe
that you were only the door
to this house where someone has suffered

and you'll keep seeking, with the final thirst,
the first well,

where something already shines inside
you, abandoning you
as you face the irresistible blinking from the depths

César Calvo
Translated by Dan Sheff

Untitled

Going through this door is easy and impossible
and only you, confidently, enter
an inferno of mirrors:
the bodies you loved and high seas are smoke, a flash
then ash, not faces erase your reflection

the brittle confusion
that you frame, word
by word, the walls of this house
you'll only leave to die

Pedro Shimose
Translated by Cola Franzen

Moxitania[1]

For César Chávez Taborga

When night shook its wings and the light woke you,
the jungle was visible in your eyes before being jungle and the river
when it was only a drop suspended in the air.

Before the guava, after the greed,
wood and water guarded your sleep.

Before fire, after tenderness,
the herons corrected their melancholy flight.

Before form—beyond touch;
before sound—beyond music;
before color—beyond light,
I loved you with my heart made of moon.

But man invaded your tale of conflagration and rainstorm,
shaped you with his hands, his fever and his alcohol,
neighing and laughter grew,
and the star-fruit tree smelled you can't imagine how much,

the jacarandas were gleaming
and the women singing on their way to the well and the mill.
Everything was soft like the breeze in the shade of the mango trees.

Now that I am far from the moment when I met you,
far
from the lightning and the flash ignorant of metal
and far
from the metal ignorant of the tropics, arrow and canoe,
I recall your face from other times,
before the almond as almond and after the *ambaibo*
as *ambaibo*.[2]
All is air redolent of balsam apple and clean clothes.

Daughter of the wind that leaves its name in every rose,
no matter that time reduced you to writing,
no matter that the orchid traded you for another city
with no flowers or birds,
no matter that the trees dried up from pure sadness,
no matter what,
how my sky-filled heart keeps on loving you!

1. Noun derived from Moxos, the land of the Indians of the same name, a region in
eastern Bolivia.—Ed.
2. Amazonian tree that bears finger-shaped clusters of fruit with a honeyed pith.—Ed.

PEDRO SHIMOSE
Translated by Cola Franzen

River of the Winds

When the fruit is a circle and erupts in a silent burst
of plumes and colors,
I flee,
        wounded by beauty,
                asking myself
who am I? Nothing perishes. (The waters add waters
and the jaguar observes us with his burning eyes.)
                Deity of another deity:
Time
listens to the memory of the rain and its green repose,
    erases

the tumults of the spume—man
lives sad with his gods
        (nothing perishes in the torpor
of the river).
      The wind
perfumes the pure instant with elder and passionflowers.
        The wind
burns in flaming roses.
      (The light fuses with the One
and fades into the birds' dreams.)
The wind looses its toucan into the orchids.
Everything is blue jubilation in the drift of the eye and its miracle.
      I go through the azaleas' glow.
Another space welcomes me with its noisy emptiness
and its lightning.
The meagerness of time.
            And its grandeur.

PEDRO SHIMOSE
Translated by Cola Franzen

Time of the Tree

1.
I saw the poem in the tropic's diaphanous night.
By starlight I read my sentiments.
You filled my mind, dream tree,
my machete,
        my serpent,
             my ardor
my young tiger heart.

"The jungle belongs to nobody," you told me, but you had a master.
Your reasoning is profound, but here there is no recourse, neither law
    nor respect. Only brute force
    drags itself along through the mud and the dead leaves, leaps
    from limb to limb, treads the black earth, sows moons in
    the rivers forever new, plunges its knife into your stem
    and nobody asks where you are, if in the root or the leaf
    or if you're called cedar or holy wood.

Everyone wanted to know you.
From top to bottom, they wanted to know you.

A king arrived on a raft bearing metals in his hands;
with death in his ax;
with death in his sling;
he navigated the waters of the Great Serpent and stopped at the ends
of the *chonta* palms and the mosquitoes.
In the shadow of delirium the Inca fled through the gray of anemia,
through the urgency of the guava tree. The sun
and the yellow trembling besieged his fortress.
The balsam apple and the *mamuri*[1] bewildered him.
And the trees loved his silence.
And the silence loved the stone.

2.
Greed arrived in long rowboats with their hubbub of boozehounds
and boors,
in the machete and the rifle with its green clangor.
Dreams!
    We were dreaming all the dreams of the world
along a river of pounds sterling.
Gold and lash in the vegetal night.
Horse in the serpent's bite.
Dog in the peccary's fangs.
Man in ants, resins and poison.
Where are the men's dreams?

Here there is rest for every wave;
silence for every affront:
shade for all fatigue.
But you were more than all that. You let yourself drift from
    green to green and laughed at human stupidity.
Your name was Fortune and everyone wanted to believe that
you were immortal.
Thus we slept peacefully, ignorant that the wreck is man's offering
to adventure.

Your freedom made those who did not love you freer still.
I would have loved you in another way.
Myself forgotten, I would have loved you: heart, springtime,
tenderness and fire.
But they loved you, to their misfortune,

and knew not what to make of your innocence, your lights,
your trills and your hives.

3.
Sonorous tree, cockcrow at daybreak,
the moon plunged into your crown and through the sky
came smoke; through smoke, fog; through the fog, the storm
    and in your branches the new country sprang up.
Sing, *ipecacuana*,[2] balsam apple and panther!
Turtles procreate on beaches lit by lightning flashes!

When all this becomes legend and even if nobody remembers your
fear and your quinine,
a tree will sing your victory on the border,
with furious southern winds claiming the future,
    my land for the world, in the love of nameless beings,
    land in the cry of your birth, tree, solely tree.

    1. The bite of the infamous *mamuri* is the most stinging of all the Amazonian mosquitoes.—Ed.
    2. The root of a small shrubby plant that possesses emetic, diaphoretic, and purgative properties.—Ed.

———————

ANÍBAL BEÇA
Translated by Alexis Levitin

Celebration
    For Tenório Telles

Nothing in the air
But Time which I am feeding.
The wind blowing by.
Consolation of absence.
Whetted blade gashing the morning.
Only it knows the scars of September.
Ancient wood creaks in the roof beam.
The clay of the tiles breathes forth moss and
geckos couple on the wall:
White upon white.
Serenity of summer thirst.
The sultry heat drinks dew from
the velvet leaves of the Caladium:

Green water jug.
Emptied of myself, I consecrate myself.

Empty.

Spectator to landscape
No one dwells within me.
And yet I consent
Replete with memory.
Pasture wherein I feed
At peace
Wheat-brown sparrow
of green meadows.
At peace?
Neither joyous nor sad.
Distant like a melody approaching.
Music of clouds.
Light
Like this poem.
Grave
A solo.
Only that. Alone.

———————

ANIBAL BEÇA
Translated by Alexis Levitin

With the Tide

For Sebastião Tapajós

It's the sea swell it's the sea smell
it's the water washing me
it's the ember sun on flesh
it's the swelling waters crashing
in that smell that smells so fresh
of the dark-skinned girl who's passing
swaying in her undulations
in the sultry rising heat

In your eyes there swims a sea
of desire hunting me;
I turn into a beast, all brazen,

hardened, rising to occasion.
A sharp and poisoned arrow hums
from hunter to the hunter's prey,
my time is here, my moment's come,
if I must die, now let it be
from passion   not from agony

———————

Anibal Beça
Translated by Alexis Levitin

Solimões

> For Célio Cruz

Acrid blade
         languid resin
citric water
       of the
           sun
               baptized solitude
                 bed of ooze
                   tongue of algae bloom

homing waves
     honing souls
razoring winds
     unraveling fish
the purling of life
              stillness of the knife
                   o
                   n

                   e
                   d
                   g
                   e
Sleek skin without wind
                   silken rest
        scarred bark swirl-wind
                   crests
On lovely lowlands

quiver of hackles
anger of winds
lesson of the waters

<pre>
                                              rush
                                     dal   ti
    dal   ti   rush   dal   ti rush   ti   dal
ti   rush dal   ti   rush dal
rush
</pre>

ANIBAL BEÇA
Translated by Nicomedes Suárez-Araúz

Haiku

In the rainy morning
the drenched ants
march on very slowly

The green fly
lands on the crimson flesh:
life for the maggots

Betrayed by his song
the cricket remains hiding
in the straw pile

Rain murmur
on the clay tile roof:
the rising moon

Sunflower in the dying day
dances in a delicate reverence
as the sun drifts away

The afternoon ravishes
with a solitary moan
sorrowful viola chords

Birds in the afternoon
carry the tune
with the flap and beat of wings

A thousand drops of light
in the rapids' rumble:
crystalline water

Yapinari[1] discovers
among water furrows
waterfall crystals

1. *Yapinari* in Nheengatu (the old Amazonian lingua franca) means "the seeing stone."—Author

---

NICOMEDES SUÁREZ-ARAÚZ
Translated by Steven Ford Brown

The following poems were taken from *Edible Amazonia*

Amazonian Orchids

Grab a little piece of dawn light
and turn it at the top so as to shape it
like a small walking stick.
Add glue to stick on
the little ball of dough
prepared beforehand.
Use this to shape the pistil.

Grab a little more dough
and touch it up with a light green color.
Shape with this piece the receptacle
which is placed as the base
of the orchid.

When the petals have been cut out
flatten them out with your fingers
and glue them around the pistil.
Paint them with light colors,
white, rose, sky blue, violet,
decorating them with a few dots and dark edges.

The flowers and the dark dwellers of the river
are always set to dry standing,
either against a slice of heaven
or a mass of green dough.

You can make them any size you wish
just by varying
the size of the pastry cutter.

The normal shape of these flowers
has three sepals and three petals
not counting the first one
which fell in 1542
when Francisco de Orellana and his army
burst into my river.

Nicomedes Suárez-Araúz
Translated by Steven Ford Brown

Leg of Wild Game

Wash the leg and scrape
any excess fat it may have.

Place it in the oven in a roasting pan.
Once it releases some of its fat
bake until it dries up and cover it
with sugar and pineapple juice.

Let it bake in a high oven
for about twenty minutes.

After removing it from the oven
cut the Indian's leg in rhomboids
and put a clove in each of them.

The rhomboids are eaten
with boiled manioc
and a slice of silence.

NICOMEDES SUÁREZ-ARAÚZ
Translated by Steven Ford Brown

Lemon Jam

To Martín Espada, defender of the downtrodden

Take ripe lemons
with a nice thick rind.
Scrape away the peel of day,
making sure no bitterness remains.

Squeeze out the juice,
leaving the rinds
free of pulp.

Place in fresh water,
changing often
in this hot climate.

To make syrup, weigh the day,
adding an equal amount of sugar,
and then place over a gentle fire.

As with all jams,
once the syrup is just right,
place lemon rinds in it,
and cook until convinced the mixture
has reached the right consistency.

Thus, each morning
the sun will rise, sweet,
with no bitterness at all,
among the Yanomami huts set ablaze
and the tribesmen
infected with fatal viruses
by the white gods.

Nicomedes Suárez-Araúz
Translated by Steven Ford Brown

Tree

To Jesús Urzagasti and Pedro Shimose, lovers of forests

Mix bread dough with water
until it turns
soft.

When ready
take a branch of lightning
that is quite resistant
and has a lovely shape
and begin to paralyze it
by using a spoon to cover it with dough,
the very same dough
with which our daily bread
was made.

Plant the branch
in a mound of dough
making sure it doesn't pass
all the way through because trees
(as the Chimane Indians know)
are also born from the sky.

When the dough has set
sprinkle with water,
until saturated.

The dough should be molded
into irregular, jutting shapes,
just like Iquitos, Leticia, Riberalta,
Manaus or Belém
as they rise in the jungle
above the river's surface.

When the branch is soaked
place in the sun
among lianas of rain
for twelve thousand years.

Then, little by little,
add to it the bark
from surrounding villages,
steamboats filled with liquid
rubber and blood;
these should be used
immediately because they dry fast
and once hardened
can no longer be used.

This is why the cycles of new life
must be added quickly:
one of *cinchona*, small,
another of rubber, large,

one of emeralds,
another of gold nuggets,

one of wood pulp,
another of oil.

As it begins to dry
continue to cover the branches
with dough, adding the new
annual buds,
always molding them into jutting shapes.

And don't forget to add the tribes,
the larger and smaller ones:
one of Xingus, another of Huitotes,
one of Muras, another of Sirionós,
one of Campas, another of Waris . . .

Better still if you mix
in the Jesuits' white plaster
for purification
and then tie up the branches
with thin wire.

Once the tree,
with its thousands of pluvial veins,
with its green tribes,
with its languages

—fragrant in spring,
bone dry in winter—
is formed,
you can brush
or dab with a cotton ball,
powdered gold paint,
making the bark light
or dark as you wish.

After the paint dries
from the sun's daily labor,
cover with copal varnish
mixed with gold dust,
giving it the desired
tonality, but leaving
no white spots.

Then with a brush in flames
begin to cover it with fire,
lighting a small flame and then another,
and another, erasing any hole it may have,
setting it ablaze as an offering to the heavens
from where the tree was born.

———————

LOS ESCRIBANOS DE LOÉN
Translated by José M. Rodeiro

Letter to Amnesia #2,089: Women [fragment]

By the road come
women with white shadows
singing the river's song,

And by the riverbank
a woman washes her clothes
washes her dark body.

Stumbling and roaring
the current comes and steals
her naked shadow,

And the woman goes away
singing with the women
of the white shadows.

LOS ESCRIBANOS DE LOÉN
Translated by José M. Rodeiro

Koma #3 ~ Nouns ~

Oar oarsman water
silence water rain oar
drowned-man water death
                oar oarsman water
woman woman clay-pitcher water
breast water bed
           oar oarsman water
kiss lung water
breath day
        eyes water
horizon bronze
          woman bones water
oar bubbles breath
        oar oarsman
death

LOS ESCRIBANOS DE LOÉN
Translated by José M. Rodeiro

Koma •#755 ~ Synonyms and Antonyms Series ~

Sorrow of an old man	Joy of a young man
who rests	who grows restless
restrained by his grief	unbound in his joy
a summing up	an expansion
sinking into darkness	emerging from light
below the never	above the always
of oblivion.	of remembrance.

Los Escribanos de Loén
Translated by José M. Rodeiro

Koma •#2,063: Loén

The hunter with his heart of hair arrived to the river stalking the most
precious preys with teeth so white they scratched the uniformity of
night the lilies bit the dark air longing to escape the night to be a vine
of white vapor to ascend up to where lilies turn into water so as to fall
as rain.

A white shadow akin to a skeleton burnt by immense distances traveled it came by the road it arrived to the bolt of winds that crisscross
Loén and it stopped its eyes a handful of keys with a great thundering
suddenly it tumbled headlong and amid the tolling of Loén's bell towers
a white moss sprouted.

In the valley so luminous the hunter and his loaded musket a call to
his love from his throat distended in an inner and white yawn the sun
with its tendons the sun at the edges of his blood as a sky and a puma
gilded by the sun yet overwhelmed by so much moonlight to the new
ark of the hunter's now gigantic hand.

The river's throat extended like the night in utterances lacking verbs
and the hunter wondered: "Who will now speak with the swollen voices
of the dead washerwomen who so often went down to the river?"

Thus the hunter with his heart of hair arrived naked to the river and
saw so many figures reflections of his very own scattered along the
valley.

The hunter felt himself to be part puma part water part tree part
night and felt himself ascending drifting with the vine of white vapor
and saw the dead washerwomen with their bodies of baked clay broken
the water of their breasts spilling as men and women part of them beast
or insect or tree or metal part of them human.

Sui-Yun
Translated by Cola Franzen

Report to Iquitos

Between the eagles' nests of walnut trees
and the raptor's counterpoint
the noisy flight encircles eyes with bloody voices

Propitious vernacular for the hunt
according to the natural laws of our rivers
dawn stripping us of our white sheets

the tamed
           ungurahuy fruit[1]
    hangs

encircled by shimmering branches
until its crèche blends into muddy or limpid waters
according to the incandescence of the day

oh strong sun that weaves my membranes
making us twins with a single babble
When you gather the limbs your legs bend the river's
innocence leaving its bed more spotless than ever!

1. *Ungurahuy:* A purple and slightly rose-colored Amazonian fruit approximately the size of a red cherry. Its alluring aroma and flavor compensate for its scant pulp.—Ed.

SUI-YUN
Translated by Cola Franzen

Untitled

At times
I sit
with my bread
surrounded by water
a few sweet peas
slipping over my eyes
scratching the corners
of my lips.

At times
I feel you so close
wounding my wings
I love you
I flee so far from you
yet the perpetual gaze
is not broken
beneath
the mirror of your eyes.

Sᴜɪ-Yᴜɴ
Translated by Cola Franzen

Untitled

They say that the wheat
threatens the sight of heaven
with the wind
and that the face of God
secretes from on high
the bounds of the Universe

To create us, vanquish us
as we rest in the shade of an old eucalyptus
our prayer of light is immersed
in the song of the everlasting leaves

Jᴜᴀɴ Cᴀʀʟᴏꜱ Gᴀʟᴇᴀɴᴏ
Translated by Frederick H. Fornoff

Healing

For Ernest Rehder

Sad Indians, burdened by memories, come to our house.

My brother, knowing how, prays and protects them
with tobacco smoke.

The Indians leave him their sadness in stones
and he turns them into clouds.

My brother earns little, but his clientele grows day by day.

Juan Carlos Galeano
Translated by Angela Ball

Herons

For Margarito Cuéllar

The fishermen who scale and gut their catch
find a river in the bellies of the fish.

In the river shines a beach where some boys play soccer.

Some herons come to the beach to take off their feathers and go for a
  swim.

The fishermen wink at the boys
urging them to bathe with the herons.

But the boys prefer to hide the herons' clothes.

Then those who scale and gut their fish
laugh so hard they fall down, choking.

The herons dress themselves in the scales of the fish and dive into the
  river.

Juan Carlos Galeano
Translated by Delia Poey

Table

For Luiz Moro

The table often dreams of having been an animal.

But if it had been an animal, it wouldn't be a table.

If it had been an animal, it would have run away like the others
when the chainsaws came to take down the trees that would become
  tables.

In the house a woman comes every night
and rubs a warm rag over its haunches as if it were an animal.

With its four legs, the table could leave the house.
But it thinks about the chairs surrounding it, and an animal would not
    abandon its family.

What the table likes best is for the woman to tickle it
as she gathers the breadcrumbs left behind by the children.

JUAN CARLOS GALEANO
Translated by Angela Ball

Kites

To Iván Oñate

Because we lacked paper to make kites, we flew our windows.

The windows with their white aprons told us what they saw.

But the Indians who saw our windows flying had neither house nor win-
    dows
to fly, let alone a kite.

It was only natural that the Indians would want to fly something.

In exchange for rotten fish, the circling vultures let strings be tied
around their necks and served as kites for the Indians.

JUAN CARLOS GALEANO
Translated by Angela Ball

Clouds

My father came to live in the Amazon to teach the Indians to make
    puzzles from clouds.

To help our father, every afternoon, my brother and I run after the idle
    clouds
passing by up there.

The clouds, like thoughts, appear and disappear.

Near our house many Indians line up to piece together puzzles
out of the clouds they know best.

Around here some clouds look like trees, and the others remind people of
 pirarucu fish.

Far off, the Indians are looking for a cloud to complete the head of an ar-
 madillo.

"With the water of our rivers and with the city games," my father writes
to his friends, "our Indians are having fun and learning to think."

My brother and I would like it better if the clouds would turn into me-
 ringues
that we could eat with milk at suppertime.

JUAN CARLOS GALEANO
Translated by Delia Poey

Eraser

> *For Roberto Fernández*

The man who needs space in his mind for important things
rubs a giant eraser on his forehead every night.

He erases many thoughts of his homeland, and every day he wakes up
with fewer square miles of memories.

His parents tell him to erase carefully, not to get so carried away
that one day he may end up erasing them, too.

The man assures them that he has a lot of practice, that he only erases
the lands and things that aren't important.

He says that he knows how to strip the trees of their leaves and let
the houses and people go untouched.

ANA VARELA TAFUR
Translated by Cola Franzen

Confession

I am a girl fearful of life.
The great monuments of the century scare me.
I do not believe in heroes born within four walls.
Officials, bureaucrats, police,
all pursue me and won't let me be. To die
at ease, to shut myself up between the thousand walls,
abode of my solitude. Listen, I do not wish to go,
do not wish to be the contemptuous girl that pretends
to disparage myself. They may burn my clothes,
follow my tracks, they will never find me. Every trace
of me has been lost between the source of my life
and the fate of the clown who amused himself with my face.
Certainly they will find me alert
in a tunnel saying outrageous things into the ears

of dogs.

ANA VARELA TAFUR
Translated by Cola Franzen

Timareo (1950)

In Timareo[1] we do not recognize letters

or writings

and nobody records us

in the official registers.

My grandfather flares up recalling the truth

about his birth
and lists a chronology surrounded

by punishments.
(There are many trees that sheltered

torture and vast groves
bought amid a thousand deaths.)
How far away the days, how distant

the flights!

The forebears sailed a sea
                    of possibilities
far from the ancestral weariness.
But we do not recognize letters or their
                              destinies
we recognize one another
          when blessed Sundays come around.
The city is far away and from the port
          I call to all the children
                    soldiers who do not return,
girls lured to movies and
                    sleazy bars.
(History does not record
our many migrations, the last voyages
launched from restless rivers.)

   1. A village in the Peruvian Amazon.—Ed.

Ana Varela Tafur
Translated by Cola Franzen

Bubble Awake in the Sea

They've closed the doors of rest.
They've opened the nearest windows of my
                              madness.
My paths trampled by storms and sharp
                    edges.
And the moon sketched on papers that demand its
                    light
While the country is a bubble awake in the
                    sea.
I'm frightened, I flee, I arise.
I am the last scarecrow awake at dawn.
And the hands that hold me just
                    collapsed.
Nobody saw me fall into the rubble, nobody.
Not one witness was among my bones.
Sundays agonize four times a month
When the city captures my destiny.
They've closed my pores,

they've not counted my minutes,
They've spread open my hands beneath the sands,
My country explodes on the banks.

ANA VARELA TAFUR
Translated by Cola Franzen

Hopeful Messages from the Sun

I'm writing a poem from you, practicing a landscape.
I sketch your orphan paths in my steps
And there are days of weeping in the ravines.
Meanwhile the young pursue better days
And brief hopeful messages from the sun
Everything is alive in me even your hillside.
Then I remember the descents without danger
And the faraway ports that make up your destiny.
I'm writing a poem from you, I'm practicing your return.

YENNY MURUY ANDOQUE
Translated by Lindsey Benitz

Beginning

We are all
humidity
If we weren't moist
if we were dry
we would not be alive

Born
in nourishing
water
We are water that settles down
receives
sustains
a yolk
a ball

playful
on this patio
this ground
in this womb
this cradle
—it stirs—
it doesn't speak, voiceless
without hands
it is all alone

I am an orphan
it says
Barely alive
it says
This is the beginning
of the pillar
of a tribal home

———————

Yenny Muruy Andoque
Translated by Lindsey Benitz

Royal Palm

Like the royal palm I am filling up with debris
filling up with dead leaves
With mere words, with stories
I am contaminated
What did I do?
Where did I lose my way?
What happened to me?

I look at my body
it seems like undergrowth
full of debris
full of centipedes
full of scorpions
spiders
ants
full of all these things

Within, inside me
my heart is well
my heart is strong
I'll survive

The palm stands up
sheds its debris
old age
filth
sickness
falseness
like mulch
she piles them
at her root

I cleanse my body
with the liquid of dawn
with the resplendent liquid of life
Further down
floating like foam
like minnows downstream my body scatters
Downstream
like driftwood it disperses

———————

Yenny Muruy Andoque
Translated by Lindsey Benitz

Navel

At first
the umbilical cord
of the owner of this world
was not cut

But that bond of light
bond of wisdom
for us
a human generation
was cut
and we were left empty

And now
we live from this world
we are nourished by the fruit of this soil

Before, we came into being
from that other nourishment
from it we drew life
it brought us light

This is our source
That is why
on these pages
I'm opening
the book that is my mother's breast
I sit, I speak
my voice is born
now my word speaks from this soil
with the names of the earth

This is my task

Prose

Fig. 2. Moacir Andrade. *A lenda da Mãe do Rio* [The Legend of the Mother of the River]. 1989. Acrylic on canvas, 110 cm x 80 cm. In the artist's personal collection. By permission of the artist.

ALFREDO FLORES
Translated by Nicomedes Austin Suárez

Sergeant Charupás

"You, One-Eye."

"Sir . . ."

The Sergeant stood at attention before the Captain, awaiting orders.

"I am holding you personally responsible for the prisoner. Is that clear? You're not to let him escape. The whole town will be after me!"

"You can count on me."

"All right, get going."

The Sergeant saluted, turned on his heels, and walked toward the door, scraping his spurs on the dusty tiles. His horse was tied to the thickest post in the corridor. He leapt onto the pale bay's back and the animal buckled under his massive weight. The Sergeant ordered his Winchester rifle to be brought to him, placed it at the front of the saddle so it would be within reach, and turned to the prisoner, who was being guarded by a soldier and awaiting departure.

"Walk in front of me," he said harshly, "and move it. We got a long road ahead of us."

They set out. The criminal, obeying the Sergeant's order, walked in front. The Sergeant followed a few steps behind, moving at the slow trot of his horse, whose clumsy gait made the dry old saddle creak.

In his heyday, Charupás had been a fort soldier in the sprawling desert between Santa Cruz and San José. There he had been hardened fighting jaguars and capturing savages. He was tall, almost a giant, black like a burnt trunk, sturdy and strong like a *guayacán* tree; he had been toughened by the sun, rains, hunger, and insects—the trademarks of the desert. In one of his raids an arrow had grazed him and he lost an eye. He dodged death only by chance. The Indian who attacked him wasn't so lucky. Charupás shot him dead, and when the man hit the ground he slashed his throat in an instant, "so you'll never forget me."

To walk safely in the forest you need good hearing and even better sight. You're always in danger if these senses are not very sharp. The one-eyed man, tired of risking his life, had thought one day of changing his line of work and accepted the Captain's invitation to assume the command of the police force, which was made up of two husk-dry, skinny soldiers.

What a peaceful life it was! Once in a while he had to shake a jolly drunk by the neck, and he had to weed the fields of the Captain who, thanks to the Sergeant, had become a modest landlord. All that aside, there was plenty of time to take pleasant naps in the delicious shade of the *cupecí* tree that stood by the wide door of the Jesuit school which had been turned into a detention office and jail, so as not to be unworthy of its old and glorious tradition.

Years would go by without a single crime that would disturb the placid life of the town which under the Captain's protective command led a quiet, sheltered existence. And whenever such crimes did occur, it was immediately necessary to move the prisoner to the closest judicial site to be locked up and judged. Any other site offered greater security than the old convent whose walls, despite their thickness, were riddled with holes, badly repaired, and inviting escape.

A few days before, at a nearby ranch, a man had brutally murdered his wife and daughter—a child of but a few months. The murderer was pursued relentlessly and was captured in spite of his desperate resistance; he barely escaped being lynched by his enraged neighbors. Because the criminal was dangerous and wily, the men voluntarily took turns guarding him while he was kept in the town's insecure prison.

To move the criminal to Santa Cruz, where he would be placed in the hands of justice, the Captain could not find a better man than Sergeant Charupás, so he entrusted him with the task, giving him all sorts of advice to prevent the prisoner from escaping en route.

They moved slowly. The sun had reached its peak, and its rays fell like lead on the heated plain. They had barely advanced two and a half leagues, and still had as much to go to finish the first day of the journey. The heat was suffocating, and it soon became necessary for them to seek shelter in the forest shadows until the sun was a little less harsh. Charupás halted his horse and approached the forest; the prisoner in turn also hurried to seek protection in the foliage so as to enjoy its freshness.

"Sit right there," said the Sergeant as he carefully set his Winchester down, "we can do with a little rest—me, the horse, and you."

The criminal made a grimace attempting a smile and, going down on his haunches, took out a few provisions from his bags. His name was Casiano Chávez. He was short, seemed almost rickety, and had a baleful and cunning look about him. A deep scar like a strap crossed his sallow face.

"That's a good one," he said and gave a sardonic little laugh as he searched painstakingly for his snack, "for you I come after that fleabag horse of yours."

The Sergeant couldn't conceal his contempt for Chávez. For that courageous black mountain of a man it was impossible to understand the cowardice of this repugnant little criminal who had brutally murdered a defenseless woman and her baby.

"So what? Do you think you're even human? For me you're worth even less than that skinny old nag!" and he pointed to the panting horse. "Don't be haughty—you've got no right to have any pride."

The prisoner tried to dismiss the Sergeant's indignation as a joke.

"You're really something, Don Charupás," he went on as he continued to eat. "Seems you're in a joking mood today."

But the black man wouldn't go along with it.

"Jokes! with you? With you, you worm? Tell me, what did you feel when you killed your wife and daughter? Didn't your heart soften when you heard their screams? You beast! Didn't you feel, if not pity, at least shame for your cowardice? Speak up, you dog!"

Chávez turned visibly pale and gave a cynical smile.

"That's none of your business," he argued. "You're not the one who's going to judge me."

Charupás shook his head spitefully. He was irked by the murderer's self-confidence and wanted to humiliate him.

"Do you have any idea of what awaits you? You think you'll escape the lead?"

"Who knows? It's happened before."

The Sergeant got up abruptly. Chávez's cynicism burned him up. He stood a moment, as though confused, then came to a decision.

"Get up—we've rested enough."

His voice sounded turbid.

He tightened his horse's cinch and mounted.

They moved at a slow pace, the prisoner up front and Charupás astride on his old bay, holding the rifle across the head of the saddle.

"Don't wander—you're not going to play games with me."

The prisoner returned to the middle of the path.

They hadn't gone very far. The sun was still very high, setting slowly down the sky's blue path. Shadows crept from under the brush adorning the roads. At some stretches, on the white sand, the recent impression of the zigzagging of a large snake chasing its prey could be seen.

The horse tripped and almost fell.

Charupás reined the horse sharply and spat out an obscenity.

"What a way to begin—and there's still fifty leagues to go!"

He watched the prisoner, who walked on lethargically. An overwhelming anger took hold of the Sergeant. He thought of how he would have to put up with that nuisance for eight more days, badly mounted, sleeping little, watchful at all times. His situation led him to recall the time he spent as a fort guard, when in skirmishes with the savages, the whites would kill dozens of them. He realized he had killed for the sake of killing since they, in any case, couldn't help themselves in doing what they did. "After all, they were barbarians."

"Don't wander, Chávez."

In the darkness of his mind the Sergeant mulled over his ideas. The savages attacked the whites *because white men charged against them without mercy. The Indians were killed wherever we found them, and sometimes we killed some that had never attacked anyone. How unlike the Christians! They were often as savage as the so-called barbarians. Just like this worm Chávez! And just because they were Christians they were sent into town to be judged and perhaps even to be set free thanks to the pull of some rotten lawyer.*

"Don't wander, Chávez, you're starting to get on my nerves." *It wasn't fair that for similar crimes there would be such a difference in treatment.*

Suddenly the prisoner came to a stop in the middle of the path.

Charupás looked at him, surprised.

"I'm tired. I'm not moving."

The black man lost his cool.

"Walk, you lazy bum."

"I don't feel like it."

Toward evening, Sergeant Charupás made his way back to town swaying with the rhythm of the tired pale bay.

The Captain, who was relaxing in the shadow of the wide eave of the corridor, tossed the cigarette butt he had between his lips and squinted his eyes.

"What the—tell me that's not Charupás."

The soldier shielded his eyes from the sun.

"Sir, it's him."

A look of complete anguish enveloped the Captain's craggy face.

"Damn it! Chávez must've escaped."

"No he's got him," the soldier said quietly, lingering in doubt.

In a moment, spurring his horse, the Sergeant approached the houses.

The Captain couldn't contain his impatience.

"Well?"

The black man dismounted and saluted.

"He tried to escape—and I shot him, Sir."

CIRO ALEGRÍA
Translated by Angela McEwan

The Call

A long cry emanated from the forest. It was a nocturnal bird that regularly announced the coming of night. The man came out of a small palm-leaf hut, stopped after a few steps, looked around with savage intensity, and said, as if in answer: "You're a little early." The sun was setting, casting golden glints on the lagoon and the tall outlines of the forest. The brilliance of the surface of the water, like polished metal, contrasted sharply with the dark shadows pooled around the tree trunks.

The trees pushed forward impetuously as if to shove the trees in front into the lagoon. Some of the large roots lay twisted at the edge of the water. Nevertheless, here and there, between the jungle and the water's edge there were some clear patches of grass. In the largest one stood the hut and that man. The palm-leaf hat was tilted up over his forehead, clearly revealing the angular outlines of his sallow face, the sharply aquiline nose, the wide lips pulled toward one side in a grimace resembling a disdainful smile. His yellowing drill shirt was stained with blood. The gray pants, cinched with a belt from which hung a machete and a revolver, bulged over low boots. He remained motionless, thumbs hooked over his belt, gallantly erect before the jungle's immensity. With his penetrating gaze, flared nostrils, sharp ears, he kept watch to see if the cry had announced something more than nightfall.

A majestic silence reigned in the calm, filled with trees and sky, beneath which, barely audible, skimming the ground, was the sound of chirping insects and the interminable croaking of tiny green toads which disappeared into the undergrowth. A sudden gust of wind ruffled the golden water and brought down a torrent of leaves. The cry rang out again in the distance.

The man returned to the hut in a few strides. The rudimentary dwelling was made up of just a curved roof on flexible poles and was one of those that jungle workers put together in a hurry, with skills learned from the savages. At the doorway, in the dying afternoon light, he set out his carbine, a rusty can of tapir grease, and a canvas knapsack that contained canned food, ropes, can openers, two cartridge belts, grease-stained rags together with others blackened by gunpowder, cartridges that matched the golden waters. He checked the loading of his weapons, having previously cleaned the barrels, and found they lacked cartridges. He began to stir the bullets in the tapir grease to protect them from corrosion produced by the dampness of the Amazon jungle. He moved his large hands as quickly as he could. Then he rubbed the bullets with a scrap of flannel to remove the excess grease and, finally, he loaded the weapons with the proper charge. His nostrils flared and he smiled at the pungent odor of greased metal and the rattling of the springs of the carbine and the revolver.

Those moments before entering the jungle and its dangers gave him a sensation of nervous pleasure. His eyes glittered like his machete, a sort of large dagger, when the bluish sheet of steel was greased in turn and almost caressed with the flannel. "Good!" he exclaimed, slashing the air joyfully.

The cry rang out again sharply, insistently, reflecting alarm. The man, who had been squatting to complete his task, stood up, putting his machete in its scabbard and then picking up the carbine which he had left leaning against the hut. He looked around again. The bird was about six furlongs away into the brush. It might have decided to cry out early, but it also might have spotted a boa, a jaguar, or a group of marauding beasts that alarmed it. It could just as easily be that a man was tracking animals or another man. It wouldn't be surprising if it turned out to be Goyo Montero. He was a bad man, and they had fought. "When you drop dead, Braulio Requena, you'll know it was me." This memory made Requena raise his carbine slightly, as if to fire. Everything was once again silent and motionless. There was not even a suspicious shadow, a shaking leaf or a single noise other than the frogs and insects, to give him reason to fire. Six furlongs take several minutes of walking in the jungle and, if it were Goyo Montero walking there, he would take a little longer to arrive. Perhaps he was following his trail and lost it at nightfall.

He missed his dog Remo, who had been eaten by a crocodile. Remo would have known right away what it was. With the bullets remaining in his knapsack Braulio Requena filled a cartridge belt and fastened it around his waist. Then he tossed the can of grease inside the hut and, after hanging the knapsack over his shoulder, he started walking with the carbine in his hands. He walked north, in the opposite direction from where the sound had come, looking back once in a while, until he reached the top of a hillock next to the lagoon.

All day long the sun had been drying eight jaguar skins which, stretched out and held in place by stakes nailed into the hard ground, looked like scars. They had a strong smell of cured leather and it was obvious that they would all be good. Two were dry enough to put inside the hut, but he decided to do it the next day. He didn't want to stay longer in the open area, where he would be an easy target.

He started toward the area where the jungle thickened. The golden color of the water was acquiring grayish tints. Where the sun was going down, the sky started to turn red. The bloodstains on his shirt were barely noticeable in the reddish light as the man disappeared among the tree trunks. Once in the jungle, the lantern light flickered and barely illuminated the shadows cast by tangled branches. After barely twenty paces, Requena turned south, toward where the cry had come from. Whether he was hunting animals or not, a man like Goyo Montero kept his Winchester and revolver fully loaded and more ammunition in the cartridge belt plus a sharp-edged machete. Although he knew that should he find Goyo attempting to fulfill his threat, the one who saw the other first would win. A single bullet would suffice.

Requena carried the carbine under his left arm and kept the knapsack under control with his right arm to keep it from banging against the tree trunks and vines, in order to avoid the slightest noise. His feet softly crushed the leaves underfoot. The bird called out again, and this time he was doing his job, as night was falling. Now sounds rang through the upper reaches of the jungle, with the rustle of leaves shaken by the wind and trills and chirps of small birds returning to their nests. An owl hooted.

Requena thought that if Goyo Montero was there, he would be hidden in those trunks that grow close together in the jungle, lying in wait, ready to shoot fast. It was exactly what could happen, but he had to face the risk as soon as possible. If Goyo planned to kill him, now or tomorrow they would have to at least meet up with each other. But neither was it a case of imagining as many possible scenarios as there were trees in the jungle. What he had to do was go forward toward whatever there was. He was comforted by the weight of his fully loaded weapons.

A sudden opening in the jungle made him go around, in order to avoid becoming an easy target again, and then he continued toward where the cry had come from. By now it wouldn't be far, and he rested his index finger lightly on the trigger. Suddenly, the peculiar shrieking cry sounded almost directly above his head. Requena stopped, pressed close to a tree, and raised the carbine. Golden shafts of sunlight barely touched a few of the tree trunks, and the deepening shadows wrapped around their roots and pressed in on the upper branches. Requena was accustomed to seeing in the dark and, in any case, he would have noticed those motionless pupils shining about fifteen feet away, inexorably fixed, piercing the darkness with murderous intent. But he didn't see them because he was looking in a different direction. There was a slithering sound. Requena turned to look and immediately distinguished the fixed points of light. Almost at that same moment he fired. It took a second bullet to put out the motionless lights. The report of the shots reverberated echoing off the gnarled tree trunks, accompanied by frantic fluttering and cries and squeaks. Requena advanced toward where the eyes were, machete in hand, because of the usefulness of the weapon in close combat. Many times, wild beasts attack, even though mortally wounded, in a final explosion of life.

Stretched out full length, an engorged boa looked like a mottled tree trunk. Requena kicked it with his foot and then slapped it with the side of the machete, but the creature didn't move. One of the bullets had hit it squarely between the eyes. The protuberance in the middle of its body indicated that the bird had cried out when it saw it crushing and swallowing. Judging from the size of the bulge, the prey had not been very large. No bigger than a peccary. "It has killed and in turn has been killed; could it happen to me too?" The hunter thought about it while looking at the length of the boa, which only minutes before was about to wrap its implacable, strangling coils around him, just as it did to the peccary or whatever it was. He whacked the nearest tree trunk with the machete to hold the sharp blade and avoid doing more damage to the reptile's skin. Now he would carefully skin it, earning a few extra soles. He specialized in hunting jaguars, but it wasn't bad to get boas also.

He put away the machete, satisfied with the outcome and that Goyo Montero wasn't around. He was free to do as he wished in the jungle, but Requena had never killed a human being. Now, more than ever, he wanted to avoid having to do so. He was even happy that Goyo Montero was not there. Requena began walking again, with the carbine in his hands, being careful not to make any noise, although not quite as carefully as before. The trails of carmine light were fading more and more in the topmost branches. Abruptly, the night closed in completely, as if growing from earth to sky.

The golden sun grew redder until it ended in shadows. In some parts of the jungle it was known as the jaguar sun, because at those moments such wild beasts, whose sensitive pupils are irritated by bright light, leave their dens and go out hunting. Requena sat down at the foot of a tree with huge branches, to eat a little and wait. He had to allow time for the jaguars, wary at first, to become completely involved in hunting, which for them was both a necessity and a violent pleasure. At such times they didn't watch out for the hunter or prepare to attack him. Their emotional desire for prey even made them go head on against a hunter. So he had to wait a little while. Requena touched the gnarled trunk of the tree next to him. In addition to the fissures due to age, it had countless little furrows where the jaguars had scratched it, leaving the marks of their sharp claws. Was it to strengthen them, were they showing off their power, or was it just a game? In any case, there was no doubt as to their hunting ability. Requena had seen them even hunt tortoises, surprising them with a tremendous head-crushing blow before they could take refuge in their shells. Also he had once seen how a jaguar caught fish. The animal was skin and bones, had probably been starving for days, and looked to be very old. Perhaps it could no longer see well at night and because of this and hunger it faced the light of day in spite of being traditionally a night hunter. Next to a stream of bluish water, leaning over as if to drink, but with one paw extended over the pool, it was waiting for a large fish it had spotted to come close enough to the edge. Just at the right moment, with a sudden slap of its paw, the jaguar knocked the fish out of the water and, before the fish had a chance to jump, snapped it up in its jaws to carry it into the jungle. Then Requena fired, although he admired jaguars in general and had watched this one sympathetically as it fished. He had to admit that jaguars even inspired his affection. That he had to kill them was another matter. And what about the strange adventure between his soul and that of a young female jaguar?

It was there in the lower Marañón, at the boundary of the Aguaruna tribe. Unconcerned about the fact that those Indians could cut off his head and shrink it, Requena began to hunt jaguars in the area. Perhaps it didn't make any difference to him. He had been through a dark period with a woman from Iquitos, while he was in the city selling pelts, and since he was much younger then, he suffered as if he were being implacably crushed. Only the direct risk to which his work exposed him helped him to forget. One day he captured a young female jaguar after killing the mother. She resembled a small tabby cat and looked at him in fright. Requena took her to his hut and fed her evaporated milk. Soon she got used to Requena, and while she grew bigger she romped joyfully and growled, sometimes sweetly and at other times as if trying to threaten him. He named her Regia, taking it from victoria regia, a hard-to-find rare jungle flower that grows in lakes and lagoons. Requena would talk to her in whispers. The tiny, warm female slept in his bed with him, and he felt less lonely. The time came when Regia could eat. Requena used his skills as never before to trap tapirs and deer and to catch fish, so that the spoiled little one should never lack fresh meat. Regia seemed to understand his efforts and repaid him by rubbing her lithe body against his legs, or his chest if he held her in his arms. At times when the sun was very bright, she would close her eyes and doze, or actually sleep, with her head resting on his arm. She was slow to wake, and while she slept, Requena did not move, pleased to have her there. He also hoped that the wild beast in her would never wake, so that she would never return to the jungle, and he even began to believe that it could never happen. On his return from hunting, he always found her in the open corridor of the cabin, or stretched out under a nearby tree. His large hands tried to be gentle when he caressed her, and Regia would stretch out with pleasure and then run and jump. In the morning and in the afternoon, when the birds sing the most, she would look at the thick jungle attentively and then come over to the man, with slow but determined steps, to rub against him in her way of being cuddly giving little growls. She didn't seem to understand about the jaguar sun, nor did she feel the need to go to the jungle. Regia grew until she was a strong adolescent. Her fur was now the right color, between yellowish and reddish, marbled with black spots. She was beautiful in her grace, soft and gentle at the same time. Her opal eyes would remain fixed on Requena for long periods and, at certain moments, they seemed to burn. To what point does a man understand or become a victim of his own thoughts? Requena believed that he could see in her looks the beginning of suspicion and even of rancor. Or at least that separation that he feared. Then, as a possible good measure, he began to dry the jaguar skins far from the hut and stored them where Regia could not see them. She remained the same, dozing contentedly or rolling around even more contentedly, rubbing up against the man to be cuddly and also looking at him in that way that began to worry him.

It seemed as if he would never notice that the killing of jaguars could be related in some way to both their lives. One day, in the afternoon, she tried out a roar. Another day, she got up and put both paws on the man's belly. Regia's attitude was undecided. But everything ended the same as always, with caresses. Except that they were given in large leaps.

One afternoon, when she finished the last hunk of tapir meat that Requena had previously cut, Regia remained waiting for him to give her more, sitting on her hind legs, looking at the man with clear hostility. This had happened several times, and Requena had held out his empty hand, telling her jokes, which made her jump and rub against him, until she invariably obtained more meat. That time it was different. When Requena held out his left hand, Regia lashed out at him with her claw, but he, being a good hunter, quickly avoided it, although she caught him on the fingertips, one of which bled. Regia tensed when she saw the blood, perhaps wanting to repeat the blow or vaguely fearful of reprisal. Wrapping the wounded hand in a handkerchief so as not to lose more blood, he picked up a leather whip with the other and went after Regia, chasing and whipping her. Overcome by pain, almost senseless, the young jaguar flattened her-

self against the ground. Requena continued lashing her, until the point
when Regia let out a cry of lamentation, part rage and part sorrow. Then
the man entered the hut, tended to his wounds with iodine and bandages,
prepared his weapons, and left to go hunting. Before entering the jungle,
he looked back and saw that Regia had sat up and was there, head lowered,
oval ears drooping. Requena felt sorry thinking that he had been too harsh
and perhaps Regia would leave. So he returned and caressed her gently on
the head, back, and flanks. Her response was not to arch her back and rub
against him as she used to do. She stretched out on the ground, head down,
growling softly. Requena wanted to pen her up but then thought that to do
so would only increase her sensation of punishment. He wasn't even sure
that on picking her up in his arms to take her to the hut that she wouldn't
scratch him again. He decided finally to go hunting, after caressing her
once again, thinking that with time she would pardon him.

When he returned the next morning with a jaguar skin, which he left,
as was his custom, far from the hut, and a red deer that he planned as a gift
for Regia, he did not find her. For many days Requena waited for the
young jaguar to return to beg for food, since she wasn't likely to be effi-
cient at hunting. From the jungle, all that came toward the hut were the
cries of animals and the sound of the wind. He still hoped to find Regia in
the jungle. He could probably recognize her by her size. Over time, the
idea that she had grown and he could kill her by mistake upset him more
than the possibility that she herself could slash his neck open with a powerful blow from her paw. Then Requena went to the Javarí River, there on
the Brazilian border, which is very far away, where he could no longer find
her.

Benjamin Sanches
Translated by Lorie Ishimatsu

the cripple

he'd never woven hammocks, stretched them out to dry, or mended the
mesh broken by the jumble of quivering fish or the teeth of the piranhas
that slipped into that swirl. that, he thought, was a wretched and tiring
practice; he always preferred to blast them. with the dynamite he could get
a better catch in less time and with less effort. but something always comes
along to strip away one's advantages, and it often comes from an empty

place where we store all our vigilance. it is life and its many faces, whose golden dust is a constant threat to us.

as he maneuvered the canoe upon reaching the mouth of the river, he felt his paddle grow heavier. he had no hands and had to hunch over in order to secure it in his arms. in this way he regained control of the canoe that had drifted slightly off course, thrust into the green gullet that restrained the mischievous waters, restless to escape their confinement. farther out, as the riverbanks grew more distant, his paddle strokes resumed that light cadence that delights the muscles and ears of those who are not unfamiliar with the beauty of music.

—i didn't know you were so nervous—he said, and turning his head astern, continued—instead of helping me paddle, you've caught your tongue on those prayers that the devil taught you. what good are those hands of yours, anyway?

an ill-humored response threatened to gather in the boy's throat, but it vanished before taking form. he decided to remain silent, although the reddening of his face revealed his disapproval of that boorish reproach.

the rottenness of the wood allowed the river to bubble into the body of the canoe, from time to time forcing them to use a gourd to bail out the water that threatened to reach the platform on which they'd placed the explosives they had prepared, along with the rest of the charges for the assault.

that task slowed their journey. his eyes brush-painted the heavens, and the position of the stars showed him that in order to reach the lake before the shoal passed, he would have to accelerate his paddle strokes that even now were furiously shredding the moon's reflection, which in these final hours of darkness insisted on lapping the mud off his oar.

three days earlier, while drinking in a floating tavern with the aid of friends, he had boasted that despite the loss of his hands, he wouldn't give up the ease of fishing with explosives, bragging endlessly of his skill in hurling them from the crook of his arm. it seemed to him that in this way he was settling scores with the devil. he had even ventured to say that were he to lose what remained of his upper limbs, he would then resort to using his feet, so as not to give up the risky profession of fish killer. everyone listened to him attentively, and some even came to admire his valiant determination; nevertheless, they always advised him to abandon his dangerous occupation, although his tiny eyes revealed to them the hatred dealt to him by his tragic fate, the memory of which he carried in his arms as a permanent vision of a clear-cut form of absence.

he had rowed more than thirty kilometers on that white moonlit night, and at that moment his powers of concentration should have been at their sharpest; yet the memory of those pleas made him nervous. it was as if those words were returning as claws that shredded his nerves while the morning mist chilled his skin.

—is the net ready?—he asked the boy.

—yes—he answered, bowing his head to make the sign of the cross.

—then straighten up and shake off your fear.

while seated he cast the first charge, which exploded in the depths without producing the desired result. it allowed only a hint of its rage to rise to the surface. jerônimo became impatient. he stood up and, after trimming the fuse of the second explosive, placed it against the end of the cigarette that was crushed between his lips; but before he could launch it in the violence of its blind fury, the stick of dynamite splintered his head and hurled his body into the water which, after displaying the man's blood, decided to conceal it forever. after tumbling through the verdant foliage, frightening the birds, the sound of the explosion faded away in the heights of that nearly deserted region.

the immaterial part of jerônimo crouched down in the prow of the canoe, enveloped in a dense smoke that spread outward and upward until it became transparent, drawing him out of his hiding place without allowing him to sense he no longer existed. though separated from his body, he hadn't lost his individuality. in thinking he existed, he came to exist in the act of thinking.

the boy who was traveling in the rear of the canoe was thrown out by the sudden shift in the air, and if not for this, fright alone would have pinned him inside the canoe. stunned, he managed to reach the shore after traversing, with great difficulty, a dense clump of foliage. still terrified in the presence of the unexpected horror, he clambered up the short slope of the riverbank and fled through the almost impenetrable thicket until, breathless, he reached the nearest homestead, which was almost four kilometers away. for the first time he was experiencing the emotion of fear in its entirety. after several minutes, free of the muteness of fatigue but still gasping for breath, he related the details of the catastrophe.—sooner or later this was bound to happen—said the black woman isaura, her eyes bulging, still swollen with sleep. she continued—he was the last one left of the traditional martins family and never wanted to get married. he had a life filled with nothing and a death everyone saw coming but benefited no one—and she concluded—he was a poor devil!

when he emerged from that fulcrum of darkness where his body struggled with death, he lived that instant without making sense of the previous minutes, without withdrawing for even a second from the life in which he'd existed. he didn't even remember hearing the explosion that had decapitated him, but perhaps recollections were of no importance to him. having lost his life, he now held eternity inside the body of his canoe. believing himself to be more alive than ever, he no longer resented the absence of his limbs. his mental processes had become more active, seeking out and creating the things he desired and taking him to live in the spiritual world, where he possessed the same emotions that had overcome him at the moment of his death. in this state he easily controlled his tangible and raw substance, since he was now attached only to a delicate thread that joined him to it.

carried away by the current, the fragile vessel drifted aimlessly, and the heavy raindrops that were accumulating in its belly threatened to capsize it. not finding the gourd, jerônimo cupped his hands to bail out the water. under the illusion that he still exists, he takes hold of the oar and begins to steer, headless and armless, accompanied by the piercing whistle of a loud ember that is attempting to escape from his headless torso.

ERASMO LINHARES
Translated by Clifford E. Landers

Beriberi

The black healer bent over the man's swollen legs and mumbled something as he removed the pipe from his mouth. In his yellowish eyes was pure grief.

"I ain't got nothin' for this sickness. It needs pharmacy drugs."

He was a tall, very thin man with the white kinky hair and the indeterminate age of older black people. The only hope and salvation of those lost in the wilderness of the rubber-tapping country. They placed their lives and their fate in those hands with enormous joints.

"I wish I could, João. But don't even think about it. I haven't been able to gather any rubber for three weeks now. And you know how the boss is. He'll say it's been six months since the health service boat was through here."

The words emerged amid distress. He was suffocating with fever. His trembling hands grasped tightly the old rags that served as blanket, spread upon the mat laid out in the middle of the thatch hut.

"Right about that. The man's a devil. But try sendin' your wife. Maybe he'll listen to her."

He observed the sick man and was startled at the great effort he made to lift his body, supporting himself on his arms. His eyes foretelling dark clouds, sunken and blackened, lingered on the old man. Yellow spittle trembled on his lips.

"No, not that," he managed to say. "He's had his eye on her for a long time."

The black man nodded but said nothing. He rose from his stool and left, bent over. When he entered the pass cut through the forest, night was approaching and little could be seen beyond the white puffs of smoke from his clay pipe.

At the foot of a nearby tree, a snipe sounded its ominous laughter as the leaves of the path were pushed aside by the sick man's wife returning from her work.

"Ana," said the tapper, opening his eyes. "The healer was here. Said there's nothing he can do. Only with medicine from the pharmacy."

The woman stood in the middle of the house. Her dark, gnat-bitten face was expressionless. She understood the situation all too well. She knew of "boss" Antoninho's intentions and of her husband's suspicions. She went outside the hut and wept silently. In her eyes, tears gleamed in the fleeing sun. She remained there for a long time. Then she went back inside, making her way through the darkness to sit on the floor at her husband's side. Fearfully, she ventured:

"What if I went and talked to the boss?"

"No!"

And he clutched the rifle lying on the floor, beneath the blanket.

Within a few days the tapper's legs were swollen cylinders, numb and unmoving. His puffy eyelids prevented him from seeing. His hands lay flat on his panting chest. The emptiness in his stomach added to his anxiety. It was late.

He was waiting for his wife. She had gone out in the morning and had not returned.

She had gone to the boss's house.

She had rowed like a madwoman. She banked the canoe at the ruffle-palm-lined beach and leapt out in front of the mud shack.

Almost at the entrance to the large door she stopped, paralyzed with fear. She stood there for an instant, thinking of the medicine and wishing to flee. She thought of the courage that had brought her this far, against her husband's will. She knew he was capable of anything. And she feared the man she was about to face. Finally deciding, she climbed the short flight of front stairs, entering the small room that served as an office.

Leaning over a crude table was "boss" Antoninho, the owner of the rubber plantation. A man with reddish, leathery skin. Grayish hair—tufts of chest hair sticking out of his open shirt. His hard, unshaven face opened in a smile when he saw her enter. He bowed grotesquely and his eyes gleamed.

"What divine favor brings you to my cabin? It's like a miracle."

"My husband," replied the terrified woman. "He's got beriberi. He needs medicine."

"Poor guy," said the man, hiding his impatience. "But things are very hard, I'm sorry. And besides everything else, he already owes me a lot. He hasn't brought me a ball of rubber for three weeks. And even if I wanted to, I couldn't. I don't have much medicine, and it's just for emergencies."

"But, Mister Antoninho . . ."

"That's it. If you really want it, you know the conditions. I can give you a little of what I have."

The woman lowered her head, rubbing her hands. Her eyes sought a point that they couldn't find.

"That's better. Let's go get the medicine, even if that shit of a husband of yours doesn't deserve anything, the lazy bastard."

And they disappeared into the depths of the cabin.

When the woman returned, her hands were full of vials and her cheeks covered with tears.

Night was falling when she moored on the riverbank. She had returned more quickly, traveling with the current. With uncertain steps she entered the hut, feeling her way along the floor, and placed the medicine beside her husband, then silently went to lean against the door. She wished she could be far away. To hide in the woods and never return. She would not succeed. A sharp cry from her husband made her tremble, overcome by anguish. She could not even feel her lips, sensing what had happened. The tapper, a vial in his hand, moaned anxiously. His body supported on one arm, he swayed and trembled.

"What's this? What've you been doing? You've been with Antoninho. You gave yourself to him like a filthy bitch."

The woman remained silent, unable to speak. Motionless and with her back turned, she was unaware that the man, gripping his rifle, was crawling toward the wall, where he propped himself up.

"You're going to die, you shameless bitch. You and him both."

The woman was paralyzed. She wanted to run, but her legs would not obey.

His finger on the trigger, wavering, suffocated by the yellow foam. He fired the weapon twice. A cry of pain penetrated the forest and was lost in the calm of night. No one had heard it.

The woman's body spun in the air, her lungs exploded, and her body thudded to the ground.

The tapper was crying now. Slowly, he began to move, dragging his legs, the rifle flung over his back. He was crying. And from time to time he laughed. Laughed and cried. Sobbed. Insane.

Supporting himself on his arms, now feeling his way, now clutching himself, he dragged his body through the dust, past the woman's lifeless body. In the cleared land outside, he stopped trying to see into the darkness around him, grinding his teeth from fever and hatred.

"You're going to die too, you pig."

He resumed the painful march along the road along the river clutching vines and bushes beside the narrow pathway. A thorn ripped his red-tinged cheek and his striped cotton shirt. His swollen legs were covered with gashes, injured by branches, cut by the serrated leaves of the razor sedge.

It was not before his body was nothing but earth and blood that he arrived at the port. He tried to descend the clay steps. Impossible. He was crying and laughing. He clutched a stake driven into the ground at the top of the ravine and launched his mutilated body into space. The shock was too much for his weakened arms. He tried to hold on, but the clay was slippery and his legs were already dead. Suddenly his fingers began to loosen, slipping rapidly.

The tapper tumbled in the air and plunged violently into the water.

The next day, vultures circled above the hut and a decaying corpse bobbed in the current.

ASTRID CABRAL
Translated by Marguerite Itamar Harrison

The Story of a Bean

He landed there by accident. Saved from the pot that was about to boil. He cursed his neighbors, those worm-eaten, degenerate beans—the harvest's castoffs—until all of a sudden he fell silent. After all, he owed them his life. By just a hair he'd been saved from that hot swirl, spared from having to

mix with a thousand other beans, from bumping up against whole toma-
toes that were like slimy buoys in a tumultuous sea.

But the earth—what a pleasure!—was moist from recent rain. I can
even see drops of rain clinging to the endive leaves, he thought contentedly. The grass is so shiny, he remarked to himself, since the others, the
spoiled beans, were dead. He was sure that for them it didn't matter that
they were on friendly turf there in the backyard, anchored in the wet, soft
earth. The cry of the bubbling water, singing from the heat, could not reach
them.

I'm going to grow up without anyone around me, he complained silently, as if sharing his thoughts with his dead companions. Then, concen-
trating all his energies, he began to survey the backyard.

He was right by the kitchen door, which scared him. Yet there wasn't
any danger because he was so small. If only he had the lively freckles of the
mulungu beans. But his color was less obvious. His somber appearance was
his armor.

Protected this way, he was able to calmly examine the guava tree
crowned with tiny flowers, as well as the trunks of other tall trees. He
couldn't see their tops. How did they grow so high? Although a bit confused, he understood how the monstrous trees and stormy skies became
one. I bet that the tops of the trees pierce the sky. That's why I can't see
them.

Exploring the backyard was entertaining. He had been confined to dark
sacks for so long that he had forgotten what it was like to be outdoors. I
swear, I was even forgetting what daylight was. So warm and clear.

While basking in the sunlight he began to recover his interrupted
past—the harvest had deprived him of light, sky, rain, and earth—and he
quietly began to swell. He experienced a sense of well being, like someone
who rediscovers himself after having been long adrift. It was true, life
could be found on earth. He was becoming whole now. After being tempo-
rarily interrupted, the link was restored, returning the original seed to the
earth. He pondered. His life, if it went on, would be easy from now on. He
yearned to fulfill his destiny, in a wave of passion for the future.

Enraptured, he remained silent in order to see, to look around him. He
was filled with tenderness for the guava blossoms. Before the guavas
started to appear he would already be a grown plant, nurturing other
beans.

Slowly he would begin extending a tiny root, a root that would gather
momentum, dragging him toward the light, to emerge, to divide, flanks
stripped of their brown garb. Having burrowed himself in the ground, us-

ing his own weight to carve out his bed in the soft soil, he would then float up to the earth's surface.

I'm alone and life's going to be tough. There's not a single experienced, grown-up bean to counsel me: "That's better." "Hey, don't be foolish." "Lean to the right." "Keep your eye on the sun." "Watch out for the ants." But how did he already know what they would say to him?

Above all, it was nice to contemplate facing the world without a single other soul to block his growth. To grow as effortlessly as taking in air. To stretch his leaves with the arrival of the sun, and relax them at night. Gently as nature taught him. With the blessing of being oblivious to reasons why. He would fulfill the tradition of his species without glorifying it. He couldn't be fooled: knowing too much is oppressive.

It was hard to see it, but he felt himself growing. Twin budding leaves opened up along the thin, sinuous stem that waved gently, sketching arcs in the air. Circular gestures unfolded in the empty space. The motion of the stem was a vain attempt to alter the indifferent vastness. He wished to attach himself to it but he recognized it as untamable, too fluid to grasp. He concluded that he was surrounded by nothingness. The air made everything slip through it; it escaped from bodies, never to be possessed.

At this very moment he was wondering about help. Who would he find to cling to? He would be forced to lay down roots when he could no longer hold himself up. He surveyed the neighborhood in search of something to lean on. He observed with great interest a snake-vine that was wrapping itself around a mango tree.

Oh, he knew how to wind around things and yet his attempts only met thin air. One day I'll walk over to the fence, grip it, and begin scaling it. I will keep stretching with time. Who knows, perhaps I'll even take over the whole fence? Right now it is completely bare and young, waiting for me. It's luring me with its fresh scent of resin.

Reluctantly, he thought, on the fence I'll be more exposed. If they don't want me there, they'll yank me out like a worthless weed. Fortunately at that point I'll already have reached a decent level of maturity; I'll be firm enough to defend myself, to impose my point of view. I won't be the pipsqueak I am now. (He nursed a little self-pity, humbled in the midst of the backyard and its resplendent lushness, where leafy trees with their thick trunks cast down a solid mantle of shade.)

But what if, in the end, they ripped him out? "What nerve! With so many pounds of beans all put up in the pantry. What a silly bean: to want to turn the whole place into a field of beans."

What if they sentenced him to become fertilizer?

Sometimes he thought about the power he had to foresee facts and things. It was as if his life just repeated itself and he never died but instead became incarnated into one period after another, carrying with him the experience of the species. He felt there was something deep inside that transcended time, allowing him to defy death's odds and to remain whole. It shared with him the secret trick to being in the world, to knowing its pitfalls and pleasures.

He wasn't surprised, then, when a stream of boiling water (the maid had the bad habit of tossing things out the window) came to gather him while, with loving care, he was mapping out his future.

José Balza
Translated by Frederick H. Fornoff

Blood

An odd-shaped coin on the counter, and not far away, that cliff. The first day he fled, hoping only to avoid capture: behind him, the disaster of his regiment and the death of the major, whose corpse had slid from the horse onto his captain, who lay motionless and covered with blood as if he were just another soldier. There he lay face down, while the protracted battle improved his chances, because nightfall would send the victors, the criollos, looking for nearby houses where they could recover from the fighting. The captain propped up the body of the major for almost five hours, and there were moments when he confused the slight pain in his own hand with the torrent of blood covering the decapitated head. At first the major's blood poured out hot and fast, covered his back, his chest; after a while it came out more slowly, porous. The decapitated body of the major grew rigid on his soldier, who experienced a vague terror rising from his gut; he shivered inwardly, as if he were being asphyxiated. In the first moment, the blood pouring from the other body into his mouth made him shudder: but he knew that any movement, any change of position would undo him: the criollos were still moving about the field. Tense, he waited for night; he would flee without anxiety because the wound in his hand seemed insignificant. He slowly swallowed the blood of the dead man and could even taste how it was getting watery and beginning to stink. Later, in the shadows, troubled and excited, he fled toward the thickets, surprised to know who he was.

On the second day, he decided the red earth would be sterile, without animals. He turned south: his wounded hand on his dagger, his steps still wary. In the afternoon, thirst overcame him; he implored; the rain lasted all night; satisfied, he let himself fall into the mud. When he opened his eyes, he discovered another man wearing a uniform like his, looking at him. He leapt up, startled. They were friends, both fleeing from the debacle. The captain had no desire to know how the other had escaped: the man's cough obsessed him.

For three days they looked for fruits and animals. The dark earth offered forests, liana vines, and fruits, the slices yellowish, sour. His own vomit enraged the captain; the other's coughing was worse. They pounded their belts with stones and ate them. Pieces of shoe leather, moistened and ground with liana leaves, made his complexion feverish. The days in that damp desert and the impenetrable nights made them dream of impossible birds, seasoned and cooked just for them. Staying awake produced a strange furor in the captain.

On the tenth day one of them made a fire and they sat down wearily. The other man was coughing weakly and threw himself down on the grass. Nervous, unerring, the captain drove his dagger into the man's back and dug out pieces of entrails. He feasted proudly, exhausted. Only afterward did he remember the embers and fire, but he was sated.

In the morning he continued toward the south. Almost immediately he came upon some straggling Indians, and he stayed with them. His hand healed; a certain taste in the vegetable diet left him feeling empty; he longed to sink his teeth into a different kind of flesh. He saw the great river possessed by the Indians. Where was he? There was nothing left of his uniform, just his white skin and newly sprouted beard. Also the dagger, an emblem of Spanish power. He practiced rowing the small native boats, purchased the company of women. But he couldn't resist: on a calm night he took two young boys and a canoe. The river absorbed them like silence. He didn't even wait until they were at a safe distance; before the sun came up he had eaten the stomach and buttocks of one boy. Half asleep, the other felt afraid.

Four days later, his hunger and thirst satisfied, austere as in former times, the soldier saw the lustrous surface of the river broken by immense stones. The mountain was descending; scattered mounds caught his attention; in a sparkling curve the river offered up the broken, commanding, symmetrical outline of a castle. The soldier doubted his senses, but in that inlet of the coast there stood a solid Spanish fortress and, at the top of the cliff, another. Excitement stirred sweet hunger in his stomach; he abandoned the boat and approached stealthily by land. In the crisp, luminous morning air, like before the outburst of rain and storm, he discovered other soldiers, his world, towers.

That same afternoon he was received and placed according to his rank. A private sobriety, a certain haughty force, invaded him as he listened to the solemn reception of the regiment. But the uniform was bothersome to him. He learned that the Spanish columns were victorious again; and yet, the following morning his first duty annoyed him, seemed unfair: he got out of bed to oversee the punishment of another soldier who had been caught trying to flee down the river a few days earlier. The captain abandoned his bed: from the patio of the castle he looked out over a horizon astonishing for its beauty and vastness; to one side the treeless savannahs; to the other, the burnished mountains; and in between, the river winding by, tumultuous, slow, deep. The captain had enveloped himself in that magnificent fortress, delicate and strategic at the same time, rising proudly in that air that burned surprisingly. But his heart would not seek its prey in the solar plenitude, would not seek there the only true water: he spun about and came to a stop before the small window of the last cell. Determined, gravely serious despite the simplicity of his task, he waited. And only then did he see, through the small opening, the framed movements of the prisoner. He was another white man, blond like himself, and naked. A bitter emptiness shook the captain: he saw the moving torso, the muscular arms, a challenge. He tried to think of some excuse, a final postponing. As if he were sleepwalking he touched his sword; then he approached the window.

But the coin made almost no noise as it fell to the counter of old wooden planks; the coin was worn thin with age, and on it the image of a castle and the date, 1813, were barely visible. We looked up toward the cliff: the ancient Spanish fortress stood there in the swift light. Castles of the Orinoco, stones of chance. The man who owned the small store picked up the coin; he only kept it to show to visitors. It was one in the afternoon; the river was getting ready for the fury, and in the distance we saw the storm that would catch us on the road. We drank the last beer. Suddenly I remembered how we had gone out in the morning toward these rapids, how we rented the boat, and how I got you interested in the distant castles. Now you've told me that it would be possible to write a story about these ruins; I smiled. What can there be behind those still steps, behind those walls with small shrubs growing from the edges? The old castles sleep; an absolute calm collects in the waters below. The beer is gone and we leave. The old man

who runs the store holds the dark coin in his hands. I look at you and smile again: our imagination is alien to the massive castles; they lack secrets; nothing, there is nothing to write about.
(1974)

César Calvo
Translated by Kenneth A. Symington

From *The Three Halves of Ino Moxo: Teachings of the Wizard of the Upper Amazon*

Prologue

Not too many years ago, when the natives of the Amazon forest were being exterminated by the rubber collectors, the chief of the Amawaka Nation, a sorcerer later famous as Ximu, the all-powerful, became aware that his people would not survive unless they were to oppose the white mercenaries with firearms, not just with lances and arrows. Since at that time it was forbidden to sell guns to natives, Ximu, the Amawaka chieftain, ordered the kidnapping of the son of a rubber collector and appointed the youth his successor, renaming him Ino Moxo, which means "Black Panther" in the Amawaka language. In that way those feared man-eaters came to be led by a white man and managed to survive. Ino Moxo, disguised in his prior identity, exchanging his Indian dress for the shirt and pants of some dead foreigner, infiltrated the cities, secured firearms, and taught Amawaka males how to use them.

When my cousin César Calvo, who was born in that region, told me the story, he made me become a part of it. Not only did he open up my curiosity while increasing his own, but also we both became captives of the same obsession: to do what no one had been able to do in over two decades—interview Ino Moxo, legendary chief of the Amawakas. With César I traveled from Lima to Pucallpa, from Pucallpa to Atalaya, and on from Atalaya, under the caprice of climate and rivers, in canoes, until we reached the territory hidden beyond the Mishawa River. During that journey we met other sorcerers—Don Javier, Don Juan Tuesta, Don Hildebrando, Juan González—and we gathered together other stories, events, and personalities, all of which began to overflow the originally intended boundaries of our report.

Even so, if someone suspects seeing in these pages anything other than just pages, I must say, as Ino Moxo said, "The miracle is in the eyes that see, not in what is seen." Because truthfully, this book is not a book. Nor a novel, nor a chronicle. It is barely a snapshot: the memories of a journey I completed while sleepwalking, magnetized by untamable forebodings and by ayahuasca, sacred drug of the Amazon sorcerers. Perhaps because of that, this story begins with my first ayahuasca visions, those images which made clear the route of our travels, the trails that Ino Moxo wished to reveal to us.

"It is unfair that people should suffer from diseases such as diabetes and several types of cancer, which are ailments we know how to stave off," said Ino Moxo when we said goodbye. "Everything that I have told you about me, about so many other things," he would say, "I have done so thinking about those people. Perhaps someone lost somewhere, without remedy, victim of a disease that doctors believe to be incurable, may read what you write and come to us and recover the joys of his existence. That is why I have told you what I have told you."

And that is why I have here joined together *the three halves*, if there is something of value in them, it is what Ino Moxo dictated to me, more through visions than through words, during the full length of a session with ayahuasca mixed with *tohé*, that other powerful and disconcerting hallucinogen.

"But I have not dictated this to you, but rather to your other self, to one of those persons inside you who surfaced during the visions—during the *mareación*. . . ."

I will only add that everything, absolutely everything contained in this text, is stored in seventeen magnetic tapes, in photographs, in the vocabulary at the end of this volume, in a booklet written by the rubber collector Zacarías Valdez, published in 1944 as "The Real Fitzcarrald in History," a copy of which I found in the library of the Maynas Municipal Council, and finally in the patience of the Green Magicians, who agreed to unveil some of their mysteries and ministries to us.

César Soriano C.
Iquitos, Peru, January 1979

We Learn that the First Man Founded the Campa Nation and Furthermore that He Wasn't a Man

"The first man was not a man—he was a woman," Don Javier tells me, entangling himself in deep laughter.

Discrete in stature, already hesitating between strength and stoutness, when Don Javier doesn't speak he laughs with his whole body and even with his shirt, printed with insolent flowers, and with his bottle-green pants, which stretch and resist. He is seated at a table in a cane chair, in this dusty bar smelling of sugarcane and tobacco and urine and beer and cheap perfumes, facing the Ucayali River, here in the outskirts of the city of Pucallpa.

No one knows how many years are hidden by Don Javier's face. His olive hands are excessively soft, as if they were gloved by a child's skin. No one knows when he began to practice, or who was (or were) his teachers. But people in the villages receive him with fiestas. They overwhelm him with consultations for sicknesses, which he diagnoses and happily cures. The young woman looking for her husband, the child possessed by a spell, lovers with unrequited love, the fisherman bitten by a viper, and the old man who coughs too much—they all have confidence in the wisdom of the amiable eyes of Don Javier. His eyes are barely more brown than his face and less brown than his lips, which are always telling stories gathered from the old wizards of the Amazon nations. They say that they place their confidence only in Don Javier—a risky confidence justifiably inaccessible to others.

"Tales that I was to learn at random, by sheer luck," he tells me, "tales I learned when my soul was young and I knew how to lose myself among the tribes and I listened quietly to all that was said, and even more quietly to what was not said. . . ."

This wandering witch doctor, given to chasing women, lacks the resignation of Don Juan Tuesta, the haughty helplessness of Don Hildebrando, and the clear enigmas of Ino Moxo. He is rather closer to Juan González in thinking of diseases as being cured by joy and not by herbs.

"It was not a man—it was a woman," he is now telling me. "And that was told to me by my Campa friend, a healer who was very famous and whose name was Inganiteri. Inganiteri in the Ashanínka language means 'it is raining.' For ten years now, Inganiteri has no longer rained. He decided to die, and to return to the earth. But shortly before that, he could inform me about the way in which human beings were first born. It was not as you may think, as you shall see. My friend Inganiteri told me that thousands of moons ago, when even the moon was only a piece of a dead trunk, in that time everything was ashes. God was not even born then, and the earth was all ashes. And light, and the stars, and air—look, air itself—and the forests, the waterfalls, the rocks, the rivers, the scrublands, the rain, the small lakes and the endless ones, and health and time and animals that creep and those that fly or walk, and the rocky places, the beaches—everything that now exists in its own way, according to its condition, what we can see, and what we do not see, everything was nothing. And that nothing itself was ashes. There was no sea; the oceans were also empty places, full of ashes. That is how the world was when suddenly lightning came down upon a pomarrosa tree. And the pomarrosa tree was ashes; it was not yet a pomarrosa. Inganiteri told me that in that instant, from that tree, that burned pomarrosa tree, which was split by lightning, a beautiful animal sprang up. The trunk of the pomarrosa opened in two, like a flower, and from the inside came the first true being. It was an animal without feathers and without scales, which did not have a memory. And the first *shirimpiáre*, the first wizard chief, who was already alive at that time even though he did not have a body (he did not have anything but was dissolved in air), the first shirimpiáre was very surprised and told himself, 'It is not a bird, not a fish, not an animal. I don't know what it may be, but it certainly is the best work of Pachamakáite.' As you know, Pachamakáite is the Father-God of the Campa. Pachamakáite is Páwa, husband of Mamántziki, son of the highest sun, the noon sun. The first shirimpiáre, then, thought for a long while and finally pronounced sentence: it must be human. That is what the number one shirimpiáre concluded after giving it thorough thought, and he decided to name that animal Kaametza. Kaametza in the Campa language means 'she, the very beautiful.' So we began with Kaametza, a female. As soon as she sprang from the pomarrosa tree, she began to search. She thought she was walking, and it was true she walked the jungle, crossing forests of cold ashes. But actually she wasn't walking; she was searching, though she did not yet know for what. Thus was Kaametza walking and searching for years and years, when one afternoon. . . ."

Don Javier pretends to look for the bottle of sugarcane brandy and refills the glass he has just emptied. I accept two sips from my glass while the sorcerer goes on talking:

"I told you 'one afternoon,' emphasizing it with the same intention that Inganiteri used with me only to be precise, so you can better see what I am remembering, because in those times there were no afternoons, no mornings or nights or noons. Time passed, but it was different from the one we know now. Time was also ashes and had no limits, like a river with three shores. Only much later did it become tame; it divided and did what the Urubamba, the sacred river of the Cusco Incas, would do at a later time. In that era, time did not get tired and lie down to rest as people do. It wasn't as it is now, cut up in pieces. Today only some sorcerers, *katziboréri*, or smoking sorcerers, shirimpiáre, are able to make that time come back, but never for more than one night or perhaps two full nights. They make it descend from the air. They bring down those pieces of time that are passing, dispersed and orphaned. They join the pieces together during many nights of concentration, after fasting two or three weeks. During those days they eat only a plantain baked over charcoal and drink only creek water. They remember, repeat, or invent the strong prayers, the magical songs, the precise *icaros*, the most appropriate and powerful invocations. Then time returns as a loving cloud or silvery pollen and again occupies the House of the Called One. Maestro Ino Moxo is one of the few shirimpiáre who have the gift of convincing time to return to its original state so that it can fulfill its first function. You should know that before, when Pachamakáite had not yet determined that Kaametza would be born, time did not serve to frame the cycle of the living. It was not its job to fix the passage of the living into the dying and the dead into what lives again in a different form, eternally. No. The first function of time was to manufacture happiness, to prevent harm in this life and in the other lives beyond. If something or someone was taken over by evil and filled up with it, time made that something or someone stop growing. It did not kill it, because death had no space in the conditions of that epoch. It just stopped it, which was worse. And simultaneously it enlarged the greatness of the great. It developed the spirits above. It gave a young spirit the experience of one thousand years. Don't forget that it had three shores—it could come and go at the same time and was quiet at the same time, fixed. The landscapes moved on both sides of it, returning and advancing toward the sea. That is why Maestro Ino Moxo, when he is under a cloud, once he has strung together those pieces of time and has made them descend, already insufflated by little silvery winds, then feeds his understanding with that ancient pollen. He multiplies the population of powers that live and work in his wisdom, fills his memory with the intelligence of thousands of lives, strengthens his power of seeing."

Only one table retaining any appearance of activity is left in the bar. There are three customers, obsessed less by the excesses of alcohol than by the disdain of that young woman with too much makeup and a dress with a low breast line, whose copious laughter presides over the ruins of this evening in front of the Ucayali River. Don Javier looks at them with mercy, with a scant disdainful curiosity that hesitates between the breasts of the woman, returns to the window, and observes nothing.

"One afternoon, then, in a creek that was also ashes, Kaametza went to see her reflection, or to drink, or to wash. She leaned over the still waters of the river coursing down these three shores, and from the heights of the jungle surged an awful panther, a black *otorongo*, bellowing. At first she remained motionless, though she was without fright. Did she know? Would she have known what fright was? What a furious otorongo was? Everything was eve and presage in the soul of Kaametza, a great dark and innocent afternoon in her understanding. Claws she could not distinguish or imagine. No words were formed in her mind, no names for anything. But thanks to that unknown knowing, the unconscious, which we still possess even today, Kaametza understood enough, and she eluded the otorongo. The otorongo again pounced upon her, its claws exposed and ready, like splinters of heated stone. And Kaametza again eluded it. Again and again the black otorongo tried to capture her, but its claws only grasped despair. And Kaametza discovered a giant fear inside of herself. She understood the closeness of death. Without thinking or attempting to do anything, she pulled a bone from her body. From in front, next to her waist—look, right here—she extracted a rib as if obeying someone, without pain or bleeding and without leaving any scar or open wound. Wielding her bone like a recently sharpened knife, she sliced through the neck of the otorongo. At this point, I remember well, my friend Inganiteri, who was telling me this story, closed his eyes and remained silent, motionless, listening. Something was coming from the depth of the woods, from the creeks that were sounding nearby, joining the waters of the Unine. We were seated at the entrance of this hut, to one side of the kaápa, the small hut he had assigned to me, on the little staircase of three thick timbers. We were looking at the forest moving in front of us, beyond a patch of cassava that marked the beginning of his property. The edge of the first sun of the afternoon was hitting the round, tamped-down patio, cleared of vegetation. But it wasn't because of the light in the patio that Inganiteri closed his eyes; it was because he spoke to me of the black panther, of that great otorongo. The face of the Campa healer aged from pure tension, increased by wrinkles on both sides of wide cheeks. After a moment he trembled. It seemed as if his soul were returning from far away, very far away, and his neck enlarged, filled with bursting veins.

"And he said that Kaametza fell to her knees after killing the otorongo. Gratefully, she knelt in the sands of ash, at the edge of that river, on its third shore, and contemplated the knife that had saved her. With her hands she brought it to her mouth slowly, very slowly, telling it things, almost kissing it, perhaps . . .

"Forgive me, Don Javier," I dare, interrupting his reverie. "Forgive me, but there is something I would like to clarify: when did chief Inganiteri close his eyes?"

"His eye," interrupts Don Javier, as is his habit. "Because Inganiteri—I don't know whether I told you—had only one eye. The other one was lost because of a wife stolen from him by Maestro Ino Moxo. He was blinded by an arrow in the midst of a war started expressly to recover her."

And he squints his eyes in the fog of the bar, against the smoke of strong tobacco and the bitter perfume of the mangos, the pomarrosas, and the yarina palms, which in the darkness overflow the borders of the Ucayali in front of us. The young woman's laughter has already deserted the neighboring back table. Don Javier bestows a condescending attention upon the three defrauded drunks.

"I'm sure he did it to remain silent," he murmurs. "I'm sure my friend Inganiteri closed his eye to keep himself from telling me any more. There he was, without seeing—he was speechless. It must be that something difficult, dangerous, forbidden to retell, perhaps must always be there in ancient stories. Speechless, then, speaking like a blind man, Inganiteri told me that Kaametza caressed her bone, perhaps lifting it to kiss it or perhaps to tell it gentle things, and the knife drawn from her body did not retain any blood from either Kaametza or from the otorongo that had scratched her. Kaametza thanked it with her breath, with the love of her mouth, gasping, and the bone was lit. It trembled like lightning you see but don't hear, lightning that knows only how to produce light. (Have you seen it? When it rains in a non-rainy season you see lightning like that.) And she released it as if it were burning her hands, and Inganiteri told me that the bone began to turn around, growing in size like a drowned man gasping for air, occupying a form that was already in the air, that has always awaited it as a destiny in the air, and which gradually resembled Kaametza more and more. It momentarily became dull and returned to brilliance, becoming the shadow of a tree on fire, a shady pomarrosa tree, the stone of an animated tree, an old footprint on a large boulder. It imitated the eyes and the arms and the hair of Kaametza, as if the body of Kaametza had always had a mold there in the air waiting for it. Then it retreated and again advanced, shining, gasping, and searching—searching for differences in the air, differentiating itself from the correspondences in Kaametza, and finally quieting down and triumphantly stretching itself upon the beach of ashes, in the darkness, identical to and different from Kaametza."

Don Javier downs in one swallow the last of the brandy in his glass and remains another moment looking at nothing, my anxiety increasing.

"That is how the male appeared. That is how we appeared. And the first shirimpiáre, who by that time already lived lifelessly without a body, and who was observing everything from the air as a witness, was happy and decided that man should live. He decided that it was good that man accompany woman and that together they should reproduce and also gave him a name. So that he could continue to exist, he gave him a name, pronouncing it loudly from the air.

"'Narowé!'" he named him.

"And the first male, hearing the name that the god Pachamakáite had approved, continued sleeping. He continued to sleep, but blood began to move all over his body and air entered his blood, impregnating his heart with the lights of generosity, spreading strength and courage over his muscles. It gave him a soul and words so that he could open the doors of the worlds, including those that cannot be seen with the eyes of the material body, so that he could be thankful to the gods and to men and so that he would know how to make war and to work and to make sons and so embellish the earth.

"'Narowé!'" he called him, which in the Campa language, in the Ashanínka language, means 'I am' or 'I am who I am.'"

The three customers at the back table have returned to drinking loudly, and they laugh and argue without noticing us. I invite Don Javier to smoke a cigarette, slowly, underlining my gesture and encouraging him to continue his story. His right hand sketches a refusal upon the palpable air of the bar, but his lips separate, are about to speak, become discouraged, and show an absent nostalgia, a half-smile. Suddenly I think I understand. I think I finally understand.

I still remember his departing smile, the obstinacy of his tight lips. Through the clouds of a strange drunkenness, however, I kept on hearing his voice. Dizzy as never before, irremediably bound to a whirlpool of hummings, heats, and shadows, I surrendered. I suspected that it was not Don Javier but the air, the voice of Inganiteri himself, already deceased, insisting in the air, who was telling me the story of Narowé and Kaametza. I broke down upon the table, abandoning my forehead over my arms. The last thing that my memory could retain from that night was the vision of my own head bent over, collapsed next to several empty bottles of brandy, as if I were to return through the arch of my crossed arms to the first moment, to the time when time was not the passive computer of the inevitable, not the builder of ruins and guide to death, but the fabricator of beauty and happiness.

I sank into an unconscious sleep as in the waters of a known and forbidden lake. The trembling of a net awakened me, dragging me back to the beach. It was not a lake; it was a river. I saw Kaametza on the third shore, luminous and naked, upon the black blood of the knifed panther, in the presence of the sleeping Narowé. I tried to approach her, but the net again captured me and returned me to waters that were ever darker, warmer, clearer. With my lost strength, nearly asphyxiated, I tried to free myself. The net enlarged, with tentacles secreting a whitish glue, and wove itself into invincible boas that surrounded me and forced me to the bottom of the waters of the river, which was now again a lake. My head came to the surface and I screamed. Nothing was heard in the air; my voice was empty. I verified that my body was also an open space, merely the location of a body. Finally sinking, with my eyes covered with salt water, I could see Kaametza on the shore, a statue absorbed before the repose of an awakening Narowé.

The boas, the net's tentacles, loosened, lied, insisted. But it was not a net. It was a hand shaking me, two hands holding my shoulders. The bar manager was waking me up with apologies—everyone had left long ago, and it was almost dawn.

I stumbled up, paid for the brandy bottles, left into a morning that began to insinuate itself from the other side of the Ucayali—its third shore— behind a double file of bamboos or perhaps bloodwoods. I do not know how I could have walked so many blocks to reach the Hotel Tariri. I only remember that in the reception lobby, pretending to look over the board hung on the wall where the room keys were placed, I was welcomed by an unvanquished smile of complicity and two open arms: Don Javier.

And We Were Granted a Meeting with the Black Panther

Ino Moxo's hut is distinguished by being different rather than large, and while we figured it would be at the center of the village, as a foundation for this dispersion of columns of smoke and huts with yellow straw sunshades, it actually occupies a timid end of it, almost out of it, on the way to the Mishawa River. And to the Mishawa we returned, sooner than we anticipated, after greeting the old chief of the Amawaka. Our hands trembled in his; our eyes did not dare meet his. We accepted a *chicha* tea made of chewed manioc and female saliva, the forced and fraternal *masato*, spiced by certain natives with a flour made of their ancestors' bones.

I don't know the exact moment when he rose from his mat, inviting us to talk by the shore of the Mishawa, as the *pona* palm structure of his hut creaked. From the other huts sad bare breasts peered timidly. Women in loincloths were behind a herd of tame trees: *chimicúas, shapájas, capironas* farther down, and behind that the face of a *sapote*, an *espintana*, three *wakapúranas*, an *ojé* of shocking green among the late clouds. I don't know at what moment we came down the three coarse steps of his house, pushed aside the *pashakula* vines framing the door, discovered a trail zigzagging to the river, and walked in a single file behind the sorcerer. We were unable to conceive that whiteness under his skin, tanned by the jungle. We were amazed at his strict Castilian pronunciation, his imperturbable drill pants under the native *cushma*, and his energetic, charmed gait, that of a wild cat—impossible if one considers the Black Panther's ninety-plus age. Now he slowed down, absorbing the sun's peace, and seated himself on the leg of a trunk devastated by fungi, dissolving his cinnamon eyes beyond the hungry hills of mahogany, bananas, and egrets and canoes piercing the shores of the river.

There is a sudden noise to my right; I turn around. A black crocodile shows himself among the trees in the muddy waters and floats closer, poorly pretending. Ino Moxo bends over and pushes him away with his hand. The enormous lizard changes course toward dusk and disappears under the bare branches of the *renaco* tree, which I only then notice in the center of the Mishawa as a sort of dead forest stripping the current with its roots drowning in the air. The Sorcerer of Sorcerers contemplates the renaco anchored in no one, helpless in the torrent, without flowers and without fruiting branches, hugged only by its own roots. He turns sadly to me, and I respond:

"Could you tell us how you became chief of the Amawakas, not being an Amawaka yourself?"

He was silent.

"Your skin is not that of a pure Indian, and you speak better than a white man."

"I am an Amawaka," he interrupted. "Very pure Amawaka. Son of a native more than of a *virakocha*, son of an Andean more than of a white man, it is true, but also a descendant of the Urus from my mother's side."

"Don Hildebrando said that you . . ."

"I am a legitimate Yora," he said, mortified. "A Yora, whom you know only as an Amawaka. Ino Moxo, that's who I am." And out of the dull neck of his cushma, the painted poncho that scares the sun and the unpredictable Amazonian downpours, he extracted from the pocket of his white shirt a crestfallen cigarette, a *shirikaipi* made of strong leaves of wild tobacco. "The problem is that I was not before what I am now," he says. "I had another name and another life before." And he lights the cigarette and the torn light tinges his profile pink. "I was not Ino Moxo before and will probably not be tomorrow." His features get lost in the fragrant, teary smoke. "It is a long story, very long—a story fully known to very few." I looked upon other kingdoms while Ino Moxo smoked, as if he were inwardly remembering, there at night on the golden edge of the Mishawa.

"You will be granted knowledge about the way in which the children devoured their parents," repeats Don Javier.

From above, upriver in the Kashpajali, erupts an end-of-afternoon sky. Almost five hundred men, more white than mestizo, have gathered with guns, with pillage, and with fear. They go downriver trying to be silent, hundreds of carbines in their hands and in boxes, and with more crates of ammunition, to the mouth of the Sutilija River, causing it to overflow with the weight of barges. Five hundred mercenaries, collected no one knows where, split currents that were recently peaceful, push waters that climb up the ankles of trees on the shore. These people are seen for the first time by this forest and the sky. The Mashko Indians who inhabit the mouth of the Sutilija River in a few houses are also surprised; they do not believe. But they already know that the virakocha, the white men, have no pity when better armed. The Mashko angrily get together, no more than twenty males, and attempt to board their canoes. Surely they intend to head to the Manu River to join their kindred and confront the virakocha in larger numbers, to throw the virakocha out of their violated territories, since the largest village of the Mashko is on the Manu, and there are three hundred invincible warriors on the Manu River. Their attempt is in vain. The astute virakocha have posted guards on both shores, and the twenty brown unarmed men cannot get through to pass the alarm. Their empty canoes float down the middle of the river. Under the red sky the water is red water.

"We had one-half hour of fierce combat," says Zacarías Valdez, one of the five hundred mercenaries. "Toward the end, we inflicted many casualties among the savages, who had to retreat in face of the energetic attitude of our combatants. The Mashko Indians lived in the Colorado River and were also spread along the shores of the Madre de Dios and the Manu Rivers, but in view of hostilities from our people, the people of the great rubber baron Fitzcarrald, they had to pull back up the Colorado River to their original territories among the headwaters of those rivers which in their language are called Piuquene, Panahua, Cumarjani, and Sutilija, all of them tributaries of the Manu. I must tell you that a distinguishing characteristic of these savages is that they are very tall and carry beards, many of them quite thick. Fitzcarrald decided to punish them and

arranged to attack their big village located some distance away down the Sutilija River. Once our personnel boarded many canoes, we set forth, and eight hundred men came ashore at the bend of the river just above the village, in order to surround it by land, giving a signal once that was completed. Meanwhile, the canoes slowly continued downriver. At four o'clock in the afternoon, we heard a heavy volley: it was the signal that fighting had begun. When we arrived at the site of the village, it was already in the hands of our people. The Mashko lost many warriors who stayed behind to defend their houses, while women and children had been moved out in time. Once the first encounter was over, the bodies were collected and cremated. Because of this funeral proceeding, the Piro Indians who were in our party named that place Mashko Rupuna, *which means 'Burned Mashko Indian.' But the fight wasn't over. We had to continue attacking the savages. The fighting was extended. Combat took place in several locations, resulting in many casualties in a war to the death, to such a degree that many bodies floated down the Manu River, and its waters were no longer potable. Finally, we dislodged the savages from the Manu, even though incompletely, because the Mashko continued their incursions, harassing our workers, until rubber extraction activities had to be discontinued in those areas, moving to other more peaceful ones."*

"It is a long, long story," says Ino Moxo. "I was thirteen years old, and at that time the chieftain of chieftains was old Ximu, a truly wise man, great and wise, giver of orders to gods and to souls."

We have barely slept the previous night, this being our second day with Ino Moxo. We breakfast on the meat of big monkeys, a species called *maquisapa*, salted and unsalted. Whole bodies are kept in a basket hanging to the side of the door of the sorcerer's hut, from which we learn they pluck a piece of leg, a joint, a shoulder, sometimes peeled like that of an adolescent, our only sustenance for four days.

Once again by the shore of the Mishawa, Ino Moxo looks at me.

"We Amawaka are few in number, very few; you have seen it. Including the ones living here, as well as those farther down in several places, we don't exceed two hundred families. Did you know that there were thousands of us in Ximu's time? The virakocha gradually exterminated us. They reduced us. They killed us only to take our lands. And they killed people of other nations as well—Jíbaros, Yaminawas, Aguarunas, Tzipíbos, Mashkos—because our lands were full of rubber, they were areas with many rubber trees, nothing but pure fat rubber roads. And the virakocha rubber men needed that rubber, they say for the progress of the country. They still say that. In the name of progress they pillaged and shot us."

And turning his face toward the renaco tree that shines in blues and oranges, erecting a labyrinth of branches against the current, in the middle of the river:

"It is a long and bitter story. If I were to tell you everything, surely you would not believe me. It is a story that is part of me, which brought me here, which rebirthed me as an Amawaka, Yora, as a Yora chief. Because my father came from Arequipa, where I was born. Where I was born the time before the last time."

"Were you then born in Arequipa?"

"The time before last."

"What do you mean?"

And he, without listening to me:

"My father came to become a rubber worker, and my mother, unwillingly, also came. As for me? I wanted to come and didn't want to. I was very young, although I think I already knew; I sniffed things, as I was to sniff destinies. Worried and happy—that is how I came, I remember. By that time, the Amawaka were already suffering too much. Whole villages died at the hands of the virakocha. It was because of it that old Ximu made me come. From the air he ordered, disposed, commanded. He brought me, as I found out later. But this story is a long one."

A young Amawaka appears to the right, among the trees to my right, carrying a black *pukuna*. He says something to Ino Moxo. Ino Moxo makes a gesture and the Amawaka speaks with Iván, who rises and says he's going to look for César and also Insapillo, to bring food. They leave me alone with the Black Panther, whose eyes wander away as he talks to the renaco, which seems to concede and makes a stand under the sun of long waters.

"Taking ayahuasca, one becomes something like a crystal," says Ino Moxo distractedly, but I am not distracted. "One becomes a crystal exposed to all the spirits, to the evil ones and the true ones that inhabit the air. That's what the icaros are for—icaros for protection—but there are also curing icaros, fundamental ones, songs that call upon a particular soul to descend and counteract other ones. With one of those icaros, Maestro Ximu made me come with his calling. He made me come as if I were a protective spirit. And before airing his icaro for me, Ximu had to fast. Because ayahuasca, like any conscious plant, has four requirements—no salt, no sugar, no fats, no sex—during all the time taken for its preparation, ingestion, and effects. Ximu had to fast so he could call me, then he ingested ayahuasca and sang the icaro. And I came. I had no choice but to obey. Because we are dealing with centuries-old wisdom, many have mistakenly died while fasting. From the time of our Uru fathers, since before the Incas, many are dead."

Under the red sky, red water. All of the mercenaries of Cumaria, Cuenga, from the Unine, sail down the Urubamba. Hundreds of canoes full of supplies, boxes and boxes of Winchester 44-caliber carbines, respond to the war call of Fermín Fitzcarrald.

"Winchesters against arrows, imagine that!" mutters the Spanish cattleman Don Andrés Rúa in Atalaya. "Repeating guns against wooden spears!"

"We were not short of fine liquors either, such as cognac and champagne," Zacarías Valdez, the rubber worker, tells us.

The expeditionaries hurry along, arrive at the landing place in the Camisea River, and come ashore. Their mestizo and Piro Indian servants take the French boxes out of the canoes, containing tinned meat and wines, and deposit them on shore. The rubber pioneers, agents of progress, have lunch, laugh, and make toasts to war— Winchesters against arrows—which they know is already won. Then they again board their canoes, leave the landing behind, go up the Manu, and arrive tired at their general headquarters at the mouth of the Kashpajali River. They arrive just in time, because a Mr. Maldonado, a representative from their leader, informs them that because of the Indians, so many dead barbarians, the rubber workers in that area have consumed their allotment of ammunition ahead of schedule.

"During that interval," says Zacarías Valdez, "since the savages insisted on attacking the rubber stations, we initiated forays against their own villages, sending hundreds of very well armed men to the Sutilija, Cumarjani, Panahua, and Pinquene Rivers, surprising the savages while they slept. Our combatants, as unequivocal proof of their actions, brought back two Indian boys as prisoners, and pieces of gold they found in those regions. Once things calmed down, and after a few days' stay in Kashpajali, a new expedition was organized. Before setting off, Fitzcarrald called together all the rubber workers and told them:

'Those who have decided never to return to their homes, step forward!'

"Of hundreds of men gathered together there, the first ones to step forward were Alfred Cockburn and Pedro Sarria, from Lima;

Erasmo Zorrilla from Ica; Carmen López from Moyobamba; and I,
Zacarías Valdez, born in Huanta, in addition to thirty Piro Indians
selected as consummate warriors.

"The guns we used were Winchester carbines, constituting the
only means of imposing the law of the strongest, which later on be-
came the law of the rubber workers.

"Well into the Madre de Dios River, we discovered a tributary to
the right, which was named the Colorado. This is what happened: we
landed somewhat above a Mashko village. The Mashkos were fierce
and tall, as I have already said, and we could not risk direct body-to-
body combat with them. They came quickly to attack us but faced
thirty gunmen firing point blank at them. Since they had never seen
guns, the loud shots of the riflemen and the death sowed in their
ranks kept them at a certain distance, from where they started shoot-
ing arrows at us. The fight lasted about two hours, and we won
thanks to our guns. The Piro warriors, able gunmen trained by us
and totally loyal to our cause, were the ones who ended the fight,
pursuing the savages to their houses and finding nothing but dead
and wounded, among which was a boy so brave that when food was
offered him he tried to bite us.

"In that place Fitzcarrald planted the Peruvian flag and baptized
the recently discovered river as the Colorado: the red river, because
its turbid waters were tinged with blood."

"This is a long story; I warned you," says Ino Moxo. "If I told you everything you would not believe me, because one can never believe everything. You can never, never listen to everything. Take, for example, the
jungle. If you try to listen to every sound in the jungle, what do you hear?
You hear more than land animals, water animals, animals of the air, even
when it is no longer possible to hear the song of the fish that gladdened the
waters of the Pangoa, Tambo, and Ucayali Rivers. Those musical beings
who foresaw the arrival of the great black otorongo fled beforehand and
saved themselves, even though they can no longer sing. Or if they do, that
is if they can still sing, they surely do it soundlessly, with notes our ears
are not accustomed to. They might sing in silence, in another dimension.
And the plants also make sounds, the stone or wood plants. Each and all
make their sound, the same as the stones.

"And more than anything else, one hears the sound of the steps of animals we have been before we were human, the sound of the steps of stones
and of plants and of things that all human beings have previously been.
And also what we have heard before, all that you can hear at night in the

jungle. Inwardly we hear, in memory, what we have listened to in the course of our lives: dances and flutes and promises and lies and fears and confessions and war cries and moans of love. True stories, stories of tomorrow—because you also hear what you will listen to in the future, what you anticipate, in the middle of the night in the jungle, in the jungle that sounds in the middle of the night. Memory is more, much more—don't you know? True memory also holds what is yet to come. And what will never come: it also holds that. Imagine. Just imagine. Who on earth could hear all of it—tell me? Who could listen to it all at once and believe it?"

Ino Moxo Says That Words Are Born, Grow and Reproduce, but Not in Spanish

"The truth is not *the* truth, but *our* truth," exclaims Maestro Ino Moxo with a hard and dark voice. "It is the truth of *oni xuma*, the truth of the *chullachaki*, the curse of Ximu!" I see him angry for the first time, breathing strongly toward the Mishawa, which slides into the night. He slightly lowers his voice.

"Ximu dedicated himself to teaching me all of our truths."

And overcome by darkness:

"I would lie if I told you that I easily adapted to Amawaka existence. I would lie if I simply told you that I adapted. In reality, it was as if I had always lived here, rising early in the morning with them, going hunting, fishing at midnight, feasting, warring, loving, cutting down trees for canoes and branches for firewood, accompanying women to capture turtles and *cupiso* eggs under the sand, learning to row without the sound of a single drop, preparing arrows and their poison, polishing blowguns, great bows, and blowing darts without letting the air know about it. And above all else, being always near Maestro Ximu, going everywhere with him, witnessing his fasts, his intoxications for invocation, of call, of exchange of knowledge, spelling out his icaros word for word, as if it were his third lip, and listening to him always. He taught me what one can know, what one should know for the benefit of human beings, of human men and things and animals, of all humans. My initial apprenticeship with Ximu lasted until I was fifteen, then it continued with other chiefs who came to teach me from afar and to practice. But at that age, the great maestro died, shortly after naming me his heir. He donned his ritual cushma when he felt death near. To enter death he donned his yellow cushma. He said farewell to me, saying nothing to the others, and he went into the forest. Ximu's body disappeared spewing smoke."

It has been four days since we arrived at Ino Moxo's village. It is almost noon. Several black lizards bask in the sun, in front of us and to our side, on the shining pebble beaches on both sides of the Mishawa. The river right at this moment is about to win; it pulls out and carries away the remains of the renaco tree downriver, to the vast and sacred Urubamba.

"Some of those things, only some of them will I tell you," says Ino Moxo slowly, gazing at the renaco, which sinks and resurfaces, stumbling, grasping the water, which dislodges it beyond the *muyuna*. "Maestro Ximu returned me to my true nation and its wisdom. He taught me that the miracle is in the eyes, in the hands that touch and search, not in what is seen, not in what is touched."

The childhood of the kidnapped boy passed in a long celebration, a noisy ceremony of potions and fierce nostalgias, in the climax of which he was re-baptized. He stretched his arms, and from the high bush his new life rained down. "Ino Moxo," said the branches above, struck by a heavy downpour. "Ino Moxo," as a talisman made of roots and darkness. Ino Moxo: Black Panther.

Enrolled in the wisdom of plants, warm animals, absent animals, things, stones, and souls; expert in conflict and in counsel; worthy of being listened to by shadows and the bodies of shadows, as Ximu intended, the kidnapped youth was to reach the loftiest depths. Disguised in his former identity, with mestizo clothes and manners, he would deceive the deceivers and obtain carbines and bullets from the white merchants. Later, returning to his real life, he would demonstrate how these iron blowguns, which spew thunder and explosions, were to be used. So Ximu ordered, and so it happened. He trained the youth starting with a first night he has never forgotten. Naked and white, among naked coppery men, surrounded by the bodies of the tribe, he received his destiny at the end of a ritual ayahuasca session.

"Visions . . . begin!" exclaimed Ximu, while calibrating the hallucinogenic apparitions in the mind of the young man, and with those two words taking over his emotions, his soul, his life. The youth learned that all barriers, all walls between his existences and those of old Ximu began to disappear. The slightest gesture of the old man developed in his consciousness the caresses of an order. Whatever Ximu thought was seen and heard by the boy. They understood each other through flashes of lightning and through shadows, amid slow visions and colors, and Ximu began to confide his patience and his strength. The boy was told which orders to accept from the souls that live in the air, which directions to ask for and listen to from ayahuasca, which intentions and operative words. He was fertilized with the capacity to carry out these orders and to transmit them, to heal bodies and souls, to mold his own life with hands of service. First of all, the youth had to learn to know dark, unclear forests in full detail, to understand the jungle, and to recognize plants one by one—their uses, spirits, and names. Because each plant has a spirit and a vocation. The same applies to animals, even the most useless ones, one by one, even those that don't exist. He started with the birds, overwhelmed by the ayahuasca, in that first Amawaka intoxication.

"Do you remember what a *panguana,* that lovely partridge, looks like?" Ximu insisted. "I want you to visualize one now, for me."

And the youth closed and opened his eyes.

"And there was the panguana!" Ino Moxo tells me with a bright smile. "There it was next to Chief Ximu and next to me—the panguana. I could see it perfectly well, tailless, with its green plumage spotted with brown. The colors of the bird were one with the reminiscences of the light, with the shades moving behind the torches, upon the leaves on the ground. I could see everything without limits. Never again in my life have I been able to see like that, with so much clarity, with so many details."

"The panguana will begin to move," Ximu alerted him.

And the panguana moved, began to turn around the youth's field of vision. Ximu invoked and produced a male panguana from the air by willing it, and the two partridges began a courtship dance, flapping their wings and gently pecking each other. A shadow appeared between the two partridges, something that made a nest on the ground, and five eggs. The male panguana sat on the five blue eggs.

"It is the male that incubates," says Ximu.

"And I saw how the eggs began to crack open!" exclaims Ino Moxo, "and from each egg grew two panguanas, big ones, adult ones!"

"It wasn't a man, it was a woman," says Don Javier to my memory. "Because the god Pachamakáite had ordered that Kaametza and Narowé were to have five . . ."

Ino Moxo interrupts him: "Later, by just gazing at Ximu's visions, I learned that there are several classes of panguanas. I learned about the trumpet birds and the *wapapas,* about many birds, all of them—all the birds. Chief Ximu went about imitating their song, and they would appear and enter my field of vision: day animals, night animals. Later they sang on their own, alone, and their songs passed into my life, forming that other part of my repertory forever. Lovely languages—I still remember them. Chief Ximu put them in my heart and my mouth in those years, in the voice of those years—my spiritual body and my material body. He taught me all the languages: the speech of the birds, the languages of the plants, the more complex ones of the stones. He taught me to tame the powers of the plants and of the stones, the dangerous and honest vocations of herbs. More than anything else he taught me to listen. He taught me to listen to them; he put my ear to their powers, their knowledge, and their ignorance, using ayahuasca. Now, if I come across a root, a flower, or a vine that Maestro Ximu did not show me in his visions, I can listen to that root, to that bush, flower, or vine. I am able to determine its soul, which solitude rules it or which company it keeps, how it was born, what it can be used for, which disease it can banish, which ills feed it. And I know with what diet, with what icaro you might increase or diminish the powers of that plant, with what songs I can nourish it, with what powerful thoughts I can graft it. The same applies to people—Chief Ximu taught me the same things about them. Something for better or worse: Ximu taught me to distinguish the days of the plants. Because on some days a plant is female and is good for certain things, and on other days the plant is male and is good for the opposite."

"If I get to a large river, I'll be safe," said the absent renaco in my vision. Later. Now, I listen to the sound of the site where its branches defied the current, and hear myself inevitably saying:

"Ayahuasca, in the Amawaka dialect—how did you say it?"

"Your question is not fair," interrupts Ino Moxo, with pity in his voice. "In the *language* of the Yoras—not a *dialect*—in their language, phrases can go away forever, join together, intermingle and separate for all time, farther away than infinity itself."

And turning his face away, nostalgic, losing himself in the absence of the renaco in the middle of the Mishawa:

"Perhaps because of the character of these jungles, this world of ours is still in its formative stage, like rivers that suddenly change course or increase or decrease their flow in a few hours. You must have seen it: if you tie down your canoe without taking it out of the water, you will find it next morning hanging in midair, if you find it at all. The river will look at you from below and you see nothing but stones, all of last night's water has been converted to stone. The reverse may also happen: your canoe may be gone with the currents, which increase without warning and give you no time to react. This world is still being formed, carving out its niche, putting in place its future, falling with the canyons. The gigantic trees, sprouting in islands that today sleep here, like the renaco, tomorrow may wake up far, far away, and in a few moments be again populated by plants, animals, people. In order to see and understand and name a world like that, we must be able to speak in that same way. A language that can decrease or ascend without warning, containing thickets of words that are here today and may wake up far away tomorrow, can in this very instant and inside the same mouth be populated with other symbols, other resonances. It will be hard for you to understand this in Spanish. Spanish is like a quiet river: when it says something, it says only what that something says. It is not so in Amawaka. In the Amawaka language, words always contain things. They always contain other words."

And with a voice that only now I recognize, Ino Moxo said, in the voice of those times in the Hotel Tariri in Pucallpa, flowing from the closed mouth of Don Javier:

"Our words are similar to wells, and those wells can accommodate the most diverse waters: cataracts, drizzles of other times, oceans that were and will be of ashes, whirlpools of rivers, of human beings, and of tears as well. Our words are like people, and sometimes much more, not simple carriers of only one meaning. They are not like those bored pots holding always the same water until their beings, their tongues, forget them, and then crack or get tired, and lean to one side, almost dead. No. You can put entire rivers in our pots, and if perchance they break, if the envelope of the words cracks, the water remains: vivid, intact, running, and renovating itself unceasingly. They are live beings who wander on their own, our words: animals that never repeat themselves and are never resigned to a single skin, to an unchanging temperature, to the same steps. And they couple, like panguanas, and have offspring.

"From the word *tiger,* coupled with the word *dance,* may be born orchids or perhaps *tohé* poison. *Night,* inseminated by *gull,* gives birth to *lightning,* a twin brother of the word that in Amawaka means 'silence-after-the-rain.' Because not just one silence exists in Amawaka, as it would in your generally quiet language, which says nothing. In Amawaka there are many silences, as there are in the jungle, as there are in our visible world, and also as many silences as exist in the worlds that cannot be seen with the eyes of the material body.

"Words, therefore, have descendants.

"And your question is unfair. I believe it comes more from virakocha prejudice than from insolence or ignorance. Even then, I will not let it go unanswered. In the Amawaka language, *ayahuasca* is *oni xuma*—write it down. But *oni xuma* does not only mean 'ayahuasca.' You shall see. *Oni xuma* may mean the same thing, or something else, or its opposite, depending on how you say it and for what purpose, depending on the time of day and the place where you say it. If I pronounce it like this—oni xuma—

with a thin voice, shining, as if spelling bonfires instead of words, in the dark, *oni xuma* means 'cutting-edge-of-flat-stone.' And pronounced another way it means 'sorrow-which-does-not-show.' And it means 'arrowhead-of-the-first-arrow.' And it means 'wound,' which also means 'lip-of-the-soul.' And always, at the same time, it is ayahuasca.

"Ayahuasca, for us, is not fugitive pleasure, venture, or seedless adventure, as it is for the virakocha. Ayahuasca is a gateway—not for escape but for eternity. It allows us to enter those worlds, to live at the same time in this and in other realities, to traverse the endless, immeasurable provinces of the night.

"That is why the light of the oni xuma is black. It doesn't explain. It doesn't reveal. Instead of uncovering mysteries, it respects them. It makes them more and more mysterious, more fertile and prodigal. Oni xuma irrigates the unknown territory: that is its way of shedding light."

. . . .

And He Orders Me to Speak from My Other Self

"It is black ayahuasca, the strongest kind," warns Don Manuel Córdova, as he pours the oni xuma mixed with tohé into a small cup, a rather yellow one, with its bottom darkened by close relatives of rust. He gets up from his couch, turns off the light, and sits down again. "Its effects will soon be noticed," he comforts us, gazing into the shadow with a serene look, to offer us confidence. All of us drink it one by one from that rusty cup. A few moments later I hear myself say something, already under the influence of the hallucinogen: a surprising whiff invades my words. It has occupied the room more as a color than as an odor, a colorless breath of dead earth, of forests handcuffed with the vine of the soul, a cold, quiet wind, a mirror raised against the forest, which the night has suddenly surrounded. I can see my voice come out of the mirror, replete with trees, and it slowly descends, like colored smoke, wrapping itself around the trunk of a *machimango* tree, then advancing to the shimmering grass that invades the floor of the open room. I close my eyes and see: we are in Don Manuel Córdova's house. Everything is all right in Huallaga Street in Iquitos. Everything is fine. The sorcerer smokes while contemplating me from the wicker sofa, and Félix Insapillo is on the floor to my right, and Iván is a little farther away, with closed eyelids, his wooden outline detailed by the fresh dim light. I hear myself repeat something. I open my eyes, the voice is mine. I'm looking at that voice, which slowly creeps toward my cousin César. But César isn't there. Only in this instant do I discover that there never was anyone in my cousin César's place. Bewildered, yet not bewildered, I look and look again at my hands and my face, I look at myself with my hands. Don Manuel Córdova teeters between compassion and satisfaction. "You're already feeling the oni xuma, aren't you?" he smiles. "It's just that this is the strongest kind. You'll know that there are two kinds of ayahuasca." His words move further away from my life; I can see them hissing in the air:

"There are two types of vine, identical on the outside, with equal color and thickness. But if you shear through their stems, you will see that one has three round strands and the other five. The black one is not any thicker, but it contains more and therefore has stronger effects."

And he rises from the *espintana* log. Everything is all right in this forest, which is no longer mirror and which occupies the room with greater conviction than a real forest. Absolutely everything is fine, smelling like a forest, sounding like a forest. Don Manuel Córdova comes across the clearing. Without surprise, I see him reach over the neck of his cushma and extract a bottle of Florida water. He unscrews the cap and the cap unfurls wings and flies away sparkling. Later he comes close and sprinkles me with the music that pours from the open bottle. The other hand of Don Manuel Córdova holds my sweating forehead. I feel fine, then I hear my cousin César, speaking through me, say that everything is all right. I feel fine, it repeats. The sorcerer wets my head with a dash of camphorated alcohol and later concentrates on the neck and chest of my brother Iván. Everything is fine. He moves to Félix Insapillo, pushing colored bamboos out of the way, *tanrilla* leg bones, *achúni* penises, a palisade of souls. He himself rubs his head, pouring drops of fragrant music through the neck opening of his cushma. The glare from torches paints, erases, paralyzes his face, his faces, those three profiles blossoming over his hair like moons, crowns of yellow and red *lupuna* leaves. I see them from a distance, far away, vanishing as I vanish.

Among the farewells of the tohé and of the night, after the stubbornness of the oni xuma, a rumor of steps, voices, movements of early risers, automobile horns penetrates the room. "How did this session go for you?" Don Manuel Córdova asks Félix Insapillo. "Well," he answers. "What visions did you have?" and Félix says: "There was a moment in which I saw my body from a distance, and I thought if someone were to whip that body sitting there, who is myself, neither it nor I would feel pain. I tried to smoke; I couldn't. I took the little box of matches and began to laugh inwardly, without my mouth laughing, because the matchbox was the skull of a deer. How could I light a cigarette with the skull of a deer, I thought, knowing that it really was a matchbox. The same with the top of that small tree next to the wall: it was a canoe that was beached there. But at the same time, in the same way, it was just the top of the small tree! Some time later, I became lost inside an enormous machine of slow colors, in the middle of huge iron gears turning noiselessly yet motionless, with pink screws, great nuts of bland colors, and pulleys. It was a fearful machine, and I was in the middle of it, in the middle of those monsters, gyrating full of yellow and violet spikes. My body was pierced by them without feeling any pain, without any bleeding."

"And my godson Iván Calvo?" asks Don Manuel Córdova. "What visions has my godson seen?" His voice—I recognize it—brings me back from the depths of the inebriation. A tiredness that doesn't belong to my body makes it collapse on the chair.

"What I have seen is not for telling," says Iván, with irritation.

Don Manuel Córdova looks at him tenderly, and still smiling turns his face to me:

"And young César Calvo, perhaps not so young? Can you tell what you have seen, or have you seen the same things as your brother Iván?"

While still stuck in my visions again, still inside the night that refuses to leave, I tell him:

"I had a very strange dream, as if I had watched a film while being drunk. At the beginning, I saw here in your living room a forest against a mirror fogged by kindness, raised against the face, against the breath of a sleeping boy. I closed my eyes and opened them, and nothing changed in the vision. Everything proceeded normally, naturally, within the dream. I dreamed that I was, and at the same time that I wasn't, and that the two of us that were I traveled from Lima to Pucallpa, and from Pucallpa to Atalaya, and I dreamed that we rented a canoe with an outboard motor in Atalaya, I dreamed that we went on the Ucayali River to the Urubamba River, and from the Urubamba to the mouth of the Inuya River. In my dream we navigated against the current several days to the Mapuya River, where we gathered marine fossils, stone shells, medusas millions of years old. I dreamed there was a man-eating wapapa, entire villages floating like fish in a poisoned lake, inside my vision."

Don Manuel Córdova pretends to fuss with his pipe, goes to light it, prefers to focus on the match he uses to remove the ashes in it. "And then?" he asks with a voice I have watched before. I decide to say nothing but fidget in the chair and don't follow my resolve:

"I saw colors, only colors, for quite a while. But the dream suddenly returned. The same dream returned and picked up where it had stopped before. We continued the journey. An Amawaka boy led us. We left the

Mapuya River behind and went into the jungle. I turned back and took aim at the wapapa with my gun. I don't know what made me change my mind. The dream kept going on with great clarity. I dreamed that I was not César Calvo but César Soriano, a cousin of mine who lives in Cajamarca: he inhabited my body, without my ceasing to be me. I lived in both persons ambling through those woods, persisting in walking next to Iván. And the boy you had sent to guide us was in front. Because I dreamed that we were walking and suffering and forcing ourselves only to be able to reach you. And I dreamed that you were the chief of the Amawaka. You were called something like Ino Moxo. Yes, I remember clearly: you were called Ino Moxo, but you were not Ino Moxo, you were Don Manuel Córdova. It was you—the light skin, the same eyes, the voice, the gestures, everything. Finally, after traversing on foot some bushy foothills, we reached the Mishawa River and you received us. Ino Moxo welcomed us, I dreamed. We spoke at length, for four days, seated on the shores of the Mishawa River. Later, without warning, coming back from an ayahuasca and tohé session identical to the one in your house tonight, Iván told me that Ino Moxo had donned his yellow cushma and entered the forest, disappearing while spewing smoke. I recall that during that inebriation, with the ayahuasca you gave me in your hut in the Mishawa, I dreamed the exact same dream I have dreamed here in your house in Iquitos, in Huallaga Street, just as if it were a dream within a dream. I had the vision of being in Atalaya with Iván, and with Félix Insapillo, and with myself—that is to say, with César Calvo—and that we navigated the Ucayali River, and the Urubamba, and the Inuya. Just as in a vision that died stillborn and never ended, like a journey ending in its beginning, which was looking at itself in my vision. Here it is still, in my head, a recently lived one, that journey that your oni xuma has made me dream."

And Don Manuel Córdova, smiling, and placing his pipe upon the side table:

"The Ashanínka say that dreaming is like conversing with the air, that during the dream one wakes up to life in another time, to one of the lives of the time of this life. What one sees with oni xuma is as real or even more real. Don't ever doubt it. Last night you really traveled, even though not in the conventional way."

And talking to himself, inwardly:

"One of the several masks of this same reality."

And his face changing, with an unforgettable voice:

"The whole journey in your dream is true for me, in my life, and it should be the same for you, a very real journey in its totality."

And weighing my doubts:

"There, on the shores of the Mishawa River, in your dream, was there a big renaco tree in the middle of the waters, or not?"

Redirecting his gestures, turning his eyes to Félix Insapillo and to my brother Iván:

"They will no longer be what they have been up to yesterday, up to the time we took oni xuma and tohé. In an imperceptible manner, but in a very real one, they too have been nourished by your visions, they have journeyed with you to their souls. Although they may not yet know it in the thinking of their hearts, beyond their memories, neither of them will ever be the same again."

And sharpening the claws of his Amawaka namesake, falling upon me from the height of his wise man's forehead:

"I know. You have not come from Lima only to have me heal your material body. And you did not come last night only to drink oni xuma mixed with tohé. I know it. That is why I dictated what you were to see in your dream. I dictated each one of the visions you saw, every one of them. That is also why I could not dictate them to you yourself, but only to your double, to one of the bodies of your shadow. Someday, if all goes well, I may confide in you. I may find out why I was not able to do it directly to you, why I made you travel inside your relative, by his side, as a stranger, why I made you travel as your other self in your visions."

The morning was becoming hot, and patients were beginning to arrive, a line of anxious and haggard faces. Abandoning the wicker sofa and saying farewells, Don Manuel Córdova gave orders that I, not César Calvo but my other César, be the one to tell, for the benefit of others, the stories of this journey I thought I had dreamed. That journey of sixty years ago, or of sixty million years in the future, in timeless time, which led me to an encounter with Ino Moxo, Black Panther of the Amawaka.

"Now go and rest," said a tired Don Manuel Córdova, sounding like a convalescent, very slowly accompanying us to the door. "But do not alter the reality of the dream; do not divorce the magic of the story or the vitality of the myth. Do not forget that rivers can exist without water but not without shores. Believe me: reality means nothing unless we can verify it in dreams."

The trembling of a net enveloped me it was not a dream it was a lake I saw Kaametza on the third shore over the black blood of the stabbed otorongo. I tried to approach her and the net returned me to the waters darker and darker warmer clearer, *qespichiway!* I shouted and it was not a lake it was a river, *qespichiway!* I invoked Kaametza, couple me with crystal let us have children who are transparent and free! the dream heard me shout that out in Quechua but did not listen, Kaametza continued on the shore absorbed and Narowé awakened, the tentacles of the net became looser, loosened lied persisted took hold of me once more. And it wasn't a net. It was a hand that was shaking me, two hands grabbing my shoulders: Roosevelt Guzmán was waking me up apologetically, saying that everyone had left the house worried about my nightmare and that it was almost dusk.

I have slept all day long, here, in this house facing July 28 Plaza, in Aguirre Street, in Iquitos, precisely in the same room where I spent my school vacations twenty years ago. The wind has not come through. I am now facing the same shutters that my father, the painter Calvo de Araújo, pushed open with fingers full of tobacco and turpentine and brushes, gathering joys and colors, and joys and angers, giving it all to the tripod where another window was waiting. Has the wind come through yet? I know very well that Don Daniel Guzmám Cepeda is not in the house, that this is no longer his house or mine, that he left together with my father, stepping on tender branches as they went, that their bodies disappeared spewing smoke. If I could only continue the dream, I say quietly, seeing, but a sudden downpour wakes me up fully. Thick drops slide down the window. I get up and close it in vain, my eyes fixed on the rain. Because the wind has come through like willows. Yes, it has come this way: mango, pomarrosa trees, devastating generous medlar trees, unforgettable eternal trees, accomplices in my life. And there is no one in the square or in the house. I ask Roosevelt to say there is no one at home, that if someone is looking for me to say that I am not at home, to tell them that I have left as well, that I left four hundred years ago. I set up a white sheet of paper, then a black one, then another white one, in the dilapidated typewriter. And I write:
THE THREE HALVES OF INO MOXO
by César Calvo

Glossary

Achúni A medium-sized, nervous, four-legged animal. Only at close range, and often only by ascertaining the hairiness of its tail and its languid ears, can one tell it apart from a fox. In spite of its well-known indifference toward chickens, the eager hunters continue to confuse them both.

Amawaka The term used to designate the Yora Nation since the Spanish conquest, as well as the natives constituting it. The main territory of the Amawakas, or Yoras, where Ino Moxo's wisdom became famous, still lies in the proximity of the Mishawa River, between the Inuya and the Mapuya Rivers, which feed the sacred river of the Incas, the grand Urubamba.

Ashanínka Name used to denote their nation by the natives who inhabit the Great Pajonal and its surroundings, an area comprising more than one hundred thousand square kilometers; they are also known as Campa.

Ayahuasca Vine-of-the-dead, vine-of-the-soul. Keshwa [Quechua] term for a hallucinogenic vine, which Humboldt renamed *Banisteriopsis caapi.*

Chullachaki From the Keshwa *ch'ullan chaki,* meaning "single foot" or "sole foot." A mythological being, a demon, a goblin. . . . In Brazil, it is known under the dubious and insolent name of *curupira.*

Espintana A straight tree, with compact bark, highly desired for beams in the construction of houses. It is known that the mother, the spirit of the *espintana,* is really two persons: an old lady and a young woman, who converse and talk at sunset.

Evil One The Evil Spirit. The greatest and most feared of all evil souls. Not *a* devil, or *a* demon, but *The Devil.*

Fitzcarrald Family name of two unforgettable genocidal criminals of the Peruvian jungle. Time and the Huaraz tongue, not yet accustomed to the English language, apparently disfigured the ancestral *Fitzgerald,* transforming it into the French-Amazonian *Fitzcarrald.* . . . The boundless ambition of Fermín and Delfín Fitzcarrald, natives of Huaraz, encouraged by the laws and authorities at the beginning of the [twentieth] century, exterminated the population of vast regions of the Amazon by blood and fire. . . .

Huapapa Wapapa, a carnivorous, web-footed, dark brown bird. With three spikes that sprout from the elbow of its wings, it tears the bark of the noxious katáwa tree, wets its feathers in the sap, flies, finds the backwater of a creek, dives in, and expertly flushes, spreads the poison in the water, and waits. On the shore, motionless, it waits for the poisoned fish to rise to the surface and then gathers them up and devours them without haste or anxiety: a piece from this one, a piece from that one. It always kills more than its appetite desires, and it does so slowly, resignedly, as if it needed to complete that premeditated, unnecessary, and bloody ceremony out of duty, not from hunger in life, but from death of satiety. The wapapa, absorbed in those trances, abstracted from everything and everyone, would be an easier hunter's prey than any of the dead fish if that were the desire of any hunter as blind as the wapapa itself. The wapapa gives the impression of being a corpse undeservedly resurrected, a sleepwalker, reduced to follow the dictates of an immemorial perversion.

Icaro Magical song.

Kaametza In the Campa language, "she, the very beautiful." The first human being, she sprang from the pomarrosa tree. From one of her bones the first male appeared and the supreme god Pachamakáite named him Narowé, which in the Campa language, in the Ashanínka language, means "I am" or "I am who I am."—*Ed.*

Machimango Tall and solid tree, recognizable by its imposing aspect as well as by the sharp, excessive perfume of its branches in fruit.

Mareación Inebriation, intoxication.

Muyuna Whirlpool, a circular current, which rivers encourage especially in their ninety-degree turns.

Narowé The first man formed from a bone of Kaametza.—Ed.

Oni xuma Ayawashka, in the Yora (Amawaka) language.

Otorongo From the Keshwa *uturunqu:* puma, tiger, panther, jaguar. Most commonly the coat of this animal tends to be yellow-green spotted with gray. The darker its color, the more it is feared. Only some humans can equal it in fierceness. This animal, therefore, is the only one that lives and dies alone.

Pachamakáite The Father-God, Páwa (great Father) of the Ashanínka Nation. Son of the highest sun, the noon sun. Husband of Mamántziki. Creator and sustainer of all that passes over or remains on the surface of the earth.

Panguana The panguana is superior to any other partridge in the South American jungles in delicacy of meat, in quality of song, and in its deceits to avoid capture.

Pukuna A blowgun.

Qespichiway In Keshwa, *qespi* is "crystal," "transparent," "pristine," and therefore "free." *Chiway* is the coupling of birds for reproductive purposes exclusively. "Qespichiway!" uttered thus, with an edge of pleading, of invocation, would literally mean "Let me couple with crystal like birds who would procreate!" . . . .

Renaco An enormous tree, with gorged branches twisted toward infinity. It grows without end at ground level until it occupies a whole forest. It is well known that the sap of the renaco is a strong coagulant.

Tohé Generic name for several solanaceous plants with hallucinogenic sap and large, marble-like, bell-shaped flowers. The most common one is *Datura speciosa*, or *Tohé mullaca*. Other varieties have been variously

called *Solanum bicolor, Cornutia odorata,* and/or *Datura insignis.*
Amazonian sorcerers add the potency of tohé to the beverages based on
the juices of ayahuasca.

Virakocha White person.—*Trans.*

Yora Member of an Amazon nation of the same name. For unknown reasons, Westerners call them Amawakas instead of Yoras.

Note: The glossary definitions were extracted from César Calvo, *The Three Halves of Ino
Moxo: Teachings of the Wizard of the Upper Amazon* (Rochester, Vt.: Inner Traditions,
1995), pp. 237–59.

Max Carphentier
Translated by R. Kelly Washbourne

The Suicide of the Blue Ant

For an hour she had waited for the ending she wanted. She had climbed to
the rose that hung over the river and lay herself down on the fringe of a
petal like one who balances on the brink of an abyss. When she got there
ten petals had already fallen on the waters, at the rate of a dying rose. Then
four more fell and they all could not sustain their lightness on the churn-
ing skin of the water, which would carry them, water-logged, to their
depths. This would be her way of dying. When the petal she was clinging to
fell, she would have, voluntarily and rosily, put an end to her destiny as a
blue ant. She would die in a flash like a rose that is lost in the void. There
were but three petals to go, hers and two more. Hers would be the first to
fall, the second, the third. Each stronger breeze that blew in the suicidal
morning, shaking the branches, scattering aromas, could bring a subtle
touch of death. A breeze could be a puff of death blowing over life. Maybe.
The blue ant knew that, and saw it and wanted it. But she would not hold
the breeze accountable, since falling is inherent to petals, inevitable, and
the decision was hers.

She had been born blue, and more than that, she *felt* blue. Blue was her
affliction. She had come into this world one summer morning much like
that one and the entire colony at the foot of the fig tree cowered in fright at
her extraordinary color. Her first impression of the world was one of
fright, fright in her mother's eyes, in the eyes of her fellow ants, workers
and chiefs of the anthill. Ants are born lucid. She remembers that after the
brief awestruck comments, all around, the commander arrived, looked at
her strangely, complained of the long work stoppage, and in authoritarian

tones showed her the ropes. She was to begin work immediately in the bowl contingent, making up the second rank of those who go out in search of food. Ants have no childhood, she thought, and I am one of them, with the difference that I have the notion and the need for childhood, plus the heaven-sent stigma on my skin.

She worked the whole summer through. Work, eat, store. The conventional expenditures of a community that only looked to the interests of productivity and the stomach. Solitude like an island surrounded by eyes on all sides. Work, eat, store. No one cared about her need to stop and look at the clouds, to comment on the greenness of the grass they trod daily, to unravel the mystery of the singing forest. She wanted to always have time to feel things deeply: she would like to make the others aware of the secretly beautiful moments that arose in their work, and that went unnoticed, like the one in which her fellow ants, carrying across a beam of light on a leaf, besides not noticing the encompassing light, unswerving and with impunity desiccated the dew that contained it. Much was seen, little felt. All looked at each other, none deeply finding each other. She was a blue ant like a word shortage, a misfit in the universe where she had been born.

Another petal fell, the one to her right, hung a second in space, and disappeared in the abyss of the stream. Will mine be the next one . . . or the last? Stoically she eyed the maelstrom, and her determination enfolded her with the serenity of the great martyrs. The hour of death's closing-in transforms living things and reveals the truth of their nature, which takes its leave in its own time. She had fulfilled her destiny and was confronting her own plentitude without regret. She would never, of her own will, deny her nature, true in deed and feeling. She had loved the colors of all the seasons, the cold weighing down the leaves and the sun hanging on the fruits: the restlessness of the roseate lizard, the precision of all things, the silent palpitation of the void and the clear word of absences. Many were the times she had descended to the deepest gallery of the anthill to hear the movement of the rocks in transformation. Long had she lived with the crumbled light of the pollen and enjoyed being the fertilizing vehicle of the nubile flowers of the valley. Pieces of fruit or wings from dead little birds, her burdens were always living burdens, for she knew of the sacrifices of the defeated jungle and the fallen architecture of a flight.

Her torment was to feel different in the flesh and in her essence, in her way of fulfilling herself. The sources of her joy and stability in the world were not identical to those of her surrounding companions. She felt alienated, the only one of her kind, a vast mystery burning in a blue form. Her full self-realization set her apart from the others, rendering her strange and undesirable in a community focused entirely on material survival. The feeling of solitude is the affirmation of inner being triumphing over appearances. She had suffered much in seeking to measure up to her sisters, to try to feel as they felt, to seek as they sought by assuming a deliberate blindness to the horizons. In the anthills superfluity prevails and nothing is seen. The effort to adapt in this way had done violence to her sense of self, and life had become meaningless and suffering. She had preferred death to continuing to feel achingly unique, penned in on all sides by fear and censure.

The next-to-last petal dropped, making the one she was on quiver, weakening even more her tenuous suspension on the stalk. The midday sun, punishing the deep red velvet, lit up the minuscule overhanging parts of the final leaf, surrounding the ant with dozens of disconsolate *sírio* flowers. The day's full force was crackling the last rose petal. It would not be long now. The blueness of her body surrounded by radiance embodied by the spirit of the valley, and all the voices of the clearing sang in her breast. It was her final joy; she had discovered that the bush was singing that way because it harbored a nest in its branches just as she now heard voices right in her heart.

The wind blew, tearing the branches from the nearest *oiticica* tree, and swept the last petal from the branch. The ant closed her eyes and felt the vertigo of the fall. The wind, though, denied it the cold plunge into the waters, for the petal poised on the abyss, conquering the chasm, then hovered over the riverbank and was blown farther and farther aloft. It rose higher than bushes, rapidly gained the highest treetops, and reaching the mountain peaks, continued rising leisurely until vanishing from sight in the heart of the low-lying blue cloud. She had not fallen in the waters: our ant had returned to the heavens.

And even today few in the valley believe that she died in the heart of a blue cloud, blue like the ant herself, stifled in clarity and descent.

Márcio Souza
Translated by George R. Shivers

God's Handwriting

Forty-eight hours later there were two bodies torn by rifle blasts. A clumsy board shack, gray and warped by sun and rain. The fools who lived in the free trade zone carried irony so far as to call that a house. There was a lot of saw grass, nettle, a papaya tree, and an ancient mango, practically bare of leaves. The house with its thatched roof must have leaked like a sieve. A stream of fetid water flowed across the potholed street, sketching a dark *mapamundi* in the dry clay. The police and reporters had parked four blocks away, some thirty meters from a labyrinth of alleys, vacant lots, and sheets drying in bamboo thickets. Along the street that people called São João, one of twenty streets with the same name in Manaus, could be seen the glorious cupola of the Amazonas Opera House, as well as two or three peaked roofs of the Baré Indians' modern capital. Everybody had been on duty for forty-eight hours. Less in the case of the inhabitants of the Japiim neighborhood. The crazy inhabitants of the free trade zone were so generous with their irony they called that a neighborhood. In ten years those soft hills separated by a ditch had seen palm groves and almost impenetrable jungle, as well as farm land and swimming holes, disappear to make way for government-subsidized housing and the slums put up by the individual initiative of migrants who arrived along with the annual floods. The subsidized housing would never be finished and was an inferno of heat and dust at noon, and at night a tropical icebox of humidity and mist. There was nothing left of the former jungle, and desert spread out in every direction from the line of shacks. During the rainy season the street turned into a mud-hole that was a veritable hog heaven for the local swine population; and in the dry season it took on the appearance of a Martian landscape with all the charm that red clay can offer, covering children and chickens alike. Only the absurdity of the free trade zone could lead the residents of Japiim to refer to those forty-eight hours as fun-filled, and that fact was evident in the dark scowl that marked the face of Commissioner Frota, the expression of a man who had had enough and was now prodding the curious bystanders with the butt of his revolver, and finally lashing out with the weapon in an attempt to disperse hundreds of women and children who were chattering away without the least attempt to understand the seriousness of a police operation and, even less, the affliction of a courageous man like Commissioner Frota. About eighty members of the military police were tagging along behind the Commissioner with the same disposition of mind. "Go back to work, laggards. Get moving. Get moving," they shouted in gruff voices, adding a few polite words, while mentally thanking God that the operation was coming to an end.

The First Body

She would have been about twenty, dressed only in lacy, lemon-yellow panties, lying face-up as she would appear in the newspaper photos. A short woman, thick in the ankles, three bullet holes in her head, her dark hair streaked with dried blood. Her body had fallen beneath a Ceará hammock, her arms were pressed against her sides, and she was lying at the back of the room. On the wall, hanging from a row of nails, were a dress, a bright yellow bra, a portrait of Dom Bosco, and another dress made of synthetic Japanese brocade. The window was open and a military policeman was trying to knock a bird-pecked papaya out of the tree with a flimsy stick.

Izabel Pimentel, who by now had been dead for five hours, had died never knowing why she had been baptized with the name Izabel Pimentel. She had died sure of only one thing, that God wrote in a crooked line. Everybody in Iauareté-Cachoeira ended up with the name Pimentel. Izabel was born in Iauareté-Cachoeira and had never escaped that fact. Her father's name was Pedro Pimentel, and her mother already bore the name Maria Pimentel when she married him. In Iauareté-Cachoeira such a situation could be a source of a lot of confusion, since no one would dare start a rumor about whether Pimentel's daughter was still a virgin or whether Pimentel knocked up his neighbor's wife, because everybody in the small city, including the person who had started the rumor, would be compromised. The result was that there was no gossip in Iauareté-Cachoeira; alas, there was nothing special about the place. You couldn't even really call it a city, except for its crazy inhabitants who would purse their lips and say they were from the city of Iauareté-Cachoeira. Izabel's father was a Baniwa Indian who spent all day drinking watered-down liquor and scratching the chigger bites on his dirty feet. But not even that could be considered a trademark unique to Izabel's father, since every man in Iauareté-Cachoeira without exception, just as his name was Pimentel, spent his days drinking watered-down liquor and scratching feet swollen with bug bites. One of Pedro's other diversions was giving Izabel's mother a sound thrashing twice a year. Once at Christmas and again on the Day of Our Lady. Izabel's mother, a Tukano Indian, had several crippled fingers as a result of her husband's semiannual tradition. Old man Pedro would get riled up at Christmas and on the Day of Our Lady, because they were the only days he got to drink brandy sent in from the State of Pará or an evil tar-like brew imported from Colombia. A few years before he had even gotten hold of a bottle of Peruvian *pisco*, which stood out in his memory.

Of course Izabel's mother's crippled hands were of no use in identifying her: every married woman was thrashed on the same dates and had hands that were just as crippled, which they held out to their daughters as a warning, every time the latter mentioned marriage. Izabel Pimentel died with every one of her fingers in perfect condition and they were even well manicured, her fingernails embellished with a stylish fingernail polish, a cheap ring on the pinky finger of her left hand. Izabel Pimentel had managed to escape marriage to a native of Iauareté-Cachoeira who most certainly would have borne the name Pimentel.

A policeman saw the ring and roughly pulled it off Izabel's finger. He examined the ring in the light and put it in a small plastic bag where there were a few other trinkets. Izabel had died the owner of a pair of round, imitation-ivory earrings, made in Taiwan, an 18-karat gold bracelet, a Seiko watch with an illuminated dial, a brass medallion with the figure of St. Dominick Sávio engraved on it, and a suspicious silver coin, besides the cheap ring snatched by the policeman. Izabel Pimentel had died much richer than all the other girls from Iauareté-Cachoeira together. Which was further proof that God truly wrote in crooked lines.

The first time that Izabel heard someone mention God's handwriting was in a conversation with her mother, while they were washing clothes by the stream. Izabel was seventeen, studying in the Salesian School at the São Miguel Mission, and was spending the holidays with her parents. Izabel wanted some money to buy magazines in São Gabriel da Cachoeira, and her mother told her not to be such a fool, that they had no money to spend on such things. The fact was they had no money to spend on anything, and the only reason they didn't starve was because she had never stopped raising chickens and carried on an active egg business with her neighbors, all without her husband's knowledge. Izabel wanted to buy those glossy magazines that came in from Rio de Janeiro filled with stories of love and photographed in beautiful mansions filled with beautiful people. In school the girls pooled their money to buy the magazines, and when they got hold of them they read them until they fell apart. The stories were rather complicated, but they always had a happy ending with the heroine's marriage. Izabel had no idea whether those fellows in expensive clothes would later start drinking watered-down liquor and beating up their blonde lovers twice a year. That wasn't so important, in any case, since the girls just liked to drool over the photos of spectacular kisses and spent hours dreaming about that strange custom of couples in love in big cities, who expressed their passion by pressing lips against lips. The kiss was not a common institution along the Rio Negro, which is why the girls got so excited, dying for some practical experience.

Until that morning, when she was washing clothes with her mother, Izabel had never kissed anybody, and all she was asking for was a paltry sum of money to buy the magazine. Her mother grumbled that that was foolishness, that money didn't grow on trees, and she wasn't about to just throw it away. Izabel started to say that if her father didn't run around drinking watered-down liquor, she could very well buy the magazine. Her mother started to forcefully pound the clothes she was washing and said things were just fine the way they were. If old Pedro were not drinking so much and were a real worker, he would of course be earning money, and they would have the wherewithal to buy what they wanted. But she knew very well that that's not the way it would be; old Pedro with money in his pockets could buy all the brandy and rotgut he wanted, and then she would get a beating every day. That's why it was better if they didn't have any money at all, because two thrashings a year were plenty, thank you. God certainly wrote in crooked lines, Izabel's mother added, and that left her completely intrigued. It was really a crooked hand that started with her father's shiftlessness, continued in his cyclical violence, left them all with days of penury, and kept her from buying a magazine and admiring the kisses of big-city lovers. A divine handwriting whose curlicues mystified her, just as the fact that her name was Izabel Pimentel did; but, for the same reason, it was a striking and crystal-clear image, one so powerful that she would never again forget it. The fact that God should produce that scrawl of a life that they were enduring in Iauareté-Cachoeira, just to keep her father from beating her mother every day, was crazy, and it struck Izabel Pimentel that everybody in her family, in the rest of the city, and maybe in all of Amazonia, was nuts. It occurred to her that perhaps even she was a misshapen letter scribbled by the divine hand.

The Uaupés River flowed in soft ripples, and the sun was intense and burning. The water was tepid, and Izabel saw some girls her own age coming along the river, kicking up a racket and lifting the torn hems of their skirts. They were very homely, their unkempt hair tumbling over their round faces, their breasts forming almost perfect cones, like her own; they were happy-go-lucky and enjoying the water lapping at their legs. At that time Izabel had no idea how plain she was and was unaware of the rustic cut of the dresses she wore. It was only later that she would discover how foolish her girlfriends were, who didn't at the very least give some care to the clothes they wore, and who had no notion at all of lipstick or shampoo for their hair. Her mother always wore a dingy and baggy white blouse, her shriveled breasts hanging loose inside it, and a navy-blue skirt that hung halfway down her scarred legs. And her crazy father wore dark shorts showing off his skinny legs and leaving nothing to the imagination when he was sitting or squatting. Those fellows squatting around a gourd full of watered-down liquor, never talking, their attention only on the liquor, were all a bunch of fools, in Izabel's opinion; and then they'd go off to collapse in their miserable hammocks and snore all night, with a bonfire sending up smoke to keep the mosquitoes away. That's why Mother Lúcia at the mission school, her eyes as green as a palm frond, would hit her on the head with a stick and call her a foolish child. Izabel Pimentel would climb the guava trees for fruit and then receive communion on a full stomach every morning, another proof of how foolish she was. Mother Lúcia would lose all patience with the girl who refused to learn to spell and could not pronounce the words of the hymn to Our Lady in proper Italian. In the classroom Mother Lúcia would call Izabel to the blackboard and react furiously when she noticed the girl licking the chalk dust off her fingers. But if Izabel was crazy, Mother Lúcia was even crazier, because she went about the Uaupés dressed in her white habit, always clean and starched, and she never bathed in the river late in the afternoons, as Father Andreotti did, and she'd never kissed anybody, despite having those palm-green eyes. A young woman like Mother Lúcia consuming herself in battling Izabel's foolishness, hitting her on the head with that stick just because she asked if kissing was good and if only the lips touched in a kiss. She spent three years in the mission, with those magazines, their pages worn so thin you could no longer contemplate the mystery of a kiss nor even read the lovers' words, all of it like God's handwriting tracing her life.

Izabel Pimentel was about to finish grade school when two things happened. The first was a matter of no importance to Izabel, since she no longer had anything to do with that wrinkled corpse, surrounded by tuberoses and four candles, laid out in the same hammock as grimy as ever and receiving, with a glassy-eyed grimace, the prayers and the cigarette smoke that the old Candomblé priest sent up simultaneously. Old man Pedro was dead, after a series of useless operations that cut off his right leg piece by piece. An infection had set in and then Father Andreotti, who had been a doctor with the Italian army during World War II, diagnosed it as a case of gangrene. He took old Pedro Pimentel to the hospital at São Gabriel da Cachoeira and, with the expertise of a military doctor, lopped off the swollen and rotting limb, gave the patient a few pats of encouragement on the shoulder, and received in return a flow of words enveloped in a vapor of alcohol and water, informing him that the treatment was useless, and that he'd soon be off, pushing somebody out of the Village of the Dead, and donating one more fish to the Uaupés River. Old Pedro, despite being a good Catholic, still believed that after he died he would have to fight for a place in the always-overcrowded Village of the Dead, and that this would result in the expulsion of someone who would be cast into the Uaupés River as a fish. Old Pedro wanted to go neither to Heaven nor to Hell, much less to Purgatory; he wanted to scramble for his place in the Village of the Dead, where he could go on drinking as much watered-down liquor as he wanted. It only took a week for old Pedro to get his wish. Izabel Pimentel was called to the hospital in São Gabriel da Cachoeira and begrudgingly prayed an entire rosary for the deceased, accompanied by Mother Lúcia. Her mother was there too, gossiping with some other women, making the contacts she would need to expand her sales of fresh eggs. The death of old Pedro, who was thirty-seven years old, did nothing to change the life of Izabel Pimentel, much less the life of Maria Pimentel. Izabel's mother, who was also thirty-seven, had no intention of ever marrying again, because she figured she had already been beaten enough to be considered a good Tukano woman.

Izabel Pimentel had no thoughts of getting married either. Her greatest interest at the moment was making a decision about a proposal she had received at school from Mother Lúcia. The proposal was bizarre, and that made it even more attractive. Mother Lúcia, who was in charge of dentistry at the São Miguel Mission, had told her that her yellowing teeth, which were otherwise in good shape, but crooked and pointed, could be extracted and replaced with a pair of dentures with sparkling white teeth, polished and perfect. Mother Lúcia had stated that in that way she would be transformed into a perfect city girl, with a smile like the girls in the movie-star magazines. Izabel Pimentel wanted to know what a kiss would feel like with those marvelous teeth that she could take out and put in whenever she wanted. She could kiss with teeth or without teeth; that's why the whole thing seemed wild to her. One night Izabel decided to stay awake listening to the music of the frogs and leafing through a photo magazine in the moonlight that filtered into the girls' dormitory. Her attention was drawn to all those teeth. She reached the conclusion that only a fool would consider those tusks she had in her mouth teeth. The next morning, to Mother Lúcia's delight, she set in motion the process that would transform her poor Indian mouth into that of a human being. With every tooth that was pulled, from back to front, she would be letting herself be transported one more time along the exotic way in which God was writing her destiny in the world. But the procedure would not be cheap; it wasn't going to be done for free. Mother Lúcia now gave Izabel Pimentel the hardest chores to do. All the dishes and pots and pans had to sparkle at the hands of Izabel Pimentel. The church's cement floor had to be scrubbed, the books dusted, and the clothes starched by Izabel's hand, so that she would have beautiful teeth inside that soft cavity her mouth was becoming. Izabel was stubborn when it came to pursuing her own desires, and now, while she occupied herself with her many chores at the mission, she amused herself spitting out on the floor the blood that would leave a salty taste as it flowed down her throat. One day Izabel heard Father Andreotti arguing violently with Mother Lúcia, calling the nun crazy, demented, and insane for pulling out her students' healthy teeth. Father Andreotti hurled all those words at Mother Lúcia in a withering voice, and Izabel could not understand what was the harm in being crazy or in wanting to give a city-girl smile to a daughter of Iauareté-Cachoeira with the last name of Pimentel. That made no difference whatever to Father Andreotti, and well-mannered Izabel stood with her mouth shut and her eyes glazed over like a dead fish when Father Andreotti called her in one afternoon and told her to sit in his lap, caressed her hair and asked her not to go to Mother Lúcia's dental office again. All Izabel could smell was the odor of the priest's cassock, and all she could see were his shiny white teeth, as she sat there without moving a muscle or registering any other reaction, pretending submission to his wishes. Izabel knew that Father Andreotti was himself crazy, not only because of what he had just said, but also because of his ideas about the mission, going around all the time with a battery-operated tape recorder, recording all the old songs and the ancient stories which the missionaries themselves had condemned as diabolical and which were obviously useless. She only regretted that he was not crazy enough for her to ask him to give her a kiss. Since he was a priest, Father Andreotti did not kiss like the young men in the movie magazines, which was really crazy in such a handsome man, and Italian to boot. So Izabel got down from Father Andreotti's lap, like a bird shaking out her feathers, crushed by his caresses, and she continued her treatments with Mother Lúcia.

Finally, with the arrival of the first Christmas without a beating for Izabel's mother, Mother Lúcia committed the supreme absurdity of commandeering an entire C-47 of the Brazilian Air Force to transport a pair of dentures from Manaus to Iauareté-Cachoeira just for her. The dentures arrived wrapped in foil and packed in a colorful box that had previously contained a digital alarm clock. Izabel Pimentel would keep that box for a long time, because on it was a beautiful and colorful illustration of a Japanese girl lying on a green lawn, caught at the moment of being awakened by a digital alarm clock and displaying lovely white teeth. At midnight mass on Christmas Eve Izabel's mouth showed off all its potential charm, when she walked into the church, and the eyes of every young girl in the congregation converged enviously on her smile. Father Andreotti, who opposed the change, might think of Izabel as a distorted and ghoulish portrait, since her teeth seemed to jump out immodestly from her pre-Columbian smile. She knew it was foolish to think that dentures could be indecent, but though no one came out and said as much, that seemed to be the general opinion around the mission, especially among the boys. If the girls were really dreaming about Izabel Pimentel's new teeth, the boys clearly found them repulsive. Clearly no young man from Iauareté-Cachoeira who honored his Pimentel surname would kiss teeth that white, much less marry a mouth that from one minute to the next could end up as empty as an old woman's. Kissing those teeth, the boys thought, would be like kissing Mother Lúcia, which would have seemed just fine to them, if the sensation of sin were not so terrible. Izabel Pimentel was immediately cut off from any relationship with the other Pimentel families, which was, of course, incredibly foolish. The result was that, without even questioning her, Izabel accepted Mother Lúcia's invitation to come and work at the Salesian School in Manaus, where a pair of dentures were of no concern. Two weeks later Izabel Pimentel would board the Air Force C-47 with nothing but a small bundle of clothes and an old copy of *Capricho* magazine. Father Andreotti boarded the plane especially to commend Izabel Pimentel to the pilot, and just before takeoff, with the plane's motors already running, he patted her on the head and told her crossly to take care of herself, not to let anybody take advantage of her, and to remember that she was a young woman and a citizen who had rights, even if she was the daughter of the late Pedro Pimentel, a Baniwa Indian.

Another Corpse

Alfredo Silva, twenty-five years old, well-formed considering his slight stature, timid and wise, brave when he was alone, and disheartened because he had been stuck with the name Catarro, was dead, and he had reached that state after coming to the conclusion that everybody in Manaus was crazy. Catarro had been the last one to be found by the police dragnet, just when he was filling his gullet with beer in a rundown pool hall in Japiim.

He had gotten up to take a piss and was unzipping his fly as he walked toward the vacant lot in back of the pool hall, when he sighted two gray military police cruisers parked on the corner, and getting out of one of them, Commissioner Frota, the bastard who had already tossed him in the clink several times before, and who liked to screw him over, even after he had served his sentence. Commissioner Frota was a lunatic, Catarro was thinking, a puny little guy, but nevertheless hated, impetuous and cruel when he was backed up by other cops and coming out of some interrogation, humble in the presence of a lawyer or whenever he was obliged to get mixed up in the domestic squabbles of the well-to-do. But in all Catarro's run-ins with Commissioner Frota, the miserable cop had been totally unbending. Based on his police experience, Commissioner Frota had come to the conclusion that he could solve all the problems of thievery in Manaus by arresting and not hesitating to use his nightstick on Catarro's back. And that conclusion was by now beginning to wear thin with Catarro, because there was never a crime or an assault anywhere in the city for which he wasn't arrested immediately, given a sound thrashing, and then without further ado, released, because Commissioner Frota was incapable of solving the simplest crime, not even a case of a stolen chicken. Even Catarro's name, which he so detested, had been celebrated by Commissioner Frota in the many interviews he gave daily to the press. And amid all the madness of the free trade zone, the only newspaper that really worked was the police paper. Catarro had become a celebrity—notwithstanding he didn't deserve his reputation—by exercising his right to steal, working as a pickpocket around the Vivaldo Lima Stadium, where he tried to grab the billfold of a Papal Nuncio dressed in all his apostolic splendor during one of the ceremonies of the Eucharistic Congress in Manaus. The robbery foiled by a nervous deacon, Catarro ended up under arrest. He told the reporters he had done what he did because he thought the Nuncio was the Pope himself, a powerful man who knew what it meant to be rich, since he owned all the churches and collected every time there was a baptism, marriage, or novena. That was pure madness on Catarro's part, since the Pope did not usually frequent the Vivaldo Lima Stadium, much less carry a plastic billfold filled with twenty one-cruzeiro notes. Catarro was forgiven by the Papal Nuncio, a kind-hearted man, who went to the police station personally to confirm the robbery and to pardon him, stating that a healthy young man like Catarro had no business picking the pocket of a Papal Nuncio under the impression that he was the Pope. The Nuncio let Catarro cool his heels in jail for twenty-four hours, then offered to pay his bail so he could start a new life when he got out. That offended Catarro, who swore he would never again rob a Papal Nuncio thinking he was the Pope. After all, he was no common beggar to walk out of jail like a fool with a wad of twenty cruzeiros in one-cruzeiro bills. The fact is that Catarro had become a celebrity, and his story even appeared as a humorous article in *Veja*, a popular magazine, although he himself never knew it.

Catarro saw Commissioner Frota get out of his car and heard him shout at him to put his hands in the air and not to make another move. Catarro was not fool enough to obey such an order and instead reached down to zipper his fly, which was open, and even though nature was calling urgently, he figured he was going to have to postpone his piss until later in some safer place. The men who were drinking beer with him in the pool hall threw themselves to the floor and Catarro heard shots firing in his direction, just as he was cutting out for a nearby water hole where two old women, who were washing their clothes, started to scream in terror. Catarro plowed through a ditch and noticed that his maroon-colored Levi's were covered with mud. Catarro didn't like going around in dirty clothes, so he had yet another reason to be furious at Commissioner Frota.

Two hours later Catarro would be dead without even having had the chance to empty his bladder. That's why his body was found sitting, a little to one side, leaning against a kitchen stool, in the middle of a pool of blood and piss. Before he could cut through the backyards and reach the house where he lived with his girlfriend, who the press referred to as a Potira or Diacuí Indian, or Izabel Pirada, and with two other partners in crime, Bacurau, a cunning lowlife from the Remédios neighborhood; and Buraco or Miss Free Trade Zone, a fag who made his living holding up taxi drivers, Catarro took the first bullet in his left thigh. He didn't know that Bacurau and Miss Free Trade Zone had already been arrested and that the body of the Potira Indian girl lay bullet-riddled and dead in the middle of the room, dressed only in the lemon-colored panties he had given her and which suited her to a T.

Catarro had also failed to realize that the military police as well as the city cops, a force a hundred men strong, were in the middle of an enormous sting operation known as Operation Free Trade Zone and had the Japiim neighborhood completely surrounded and sealed off. For the last forty-eight hours, the cops of both varieties had everyone in the neighborhood all stirred up, since they wouldn't let anybody do his job in peace with all their running around in the middle of everything, as if Operation Free Trade Zone were some kind of folk festival or the devil knew what. Operation Free Trade Zone was Commissioner Frota's latest brainchild. He had managed to convince the Secretary of Public Safety to authorize a battalion of military police to surround the whole Japiim neighborhood, because he had had a dream in which there in the middle of all those wood and thatch shacks, he saw the gangsters who had carried out a holdup on the armored car that was carrying the payroll of Isagawa of the Amazon Radio Company, and in the process had killed the driver at point-blank range, just a kid from Três Corações, the same place Pelé was from. In a moment of madness, the kid had come to Manaus to contribute with his own labor to the progress of the free trade zone. It had been a brutal crime and the twentieth holdup involving a fatality in less than a week, a fact that had the population in a panic and the police with their backs against the wall. It's clear that neither Catarro, nor the Potira Indian girl, nor Bacurau nor Miss Free Trade Zone were implicated in the holdup of the Isagawa armored car. No one had the slightest doubt about that, not even Commissioner Frota. But in a city where, proportionately, more robberies took place than in New York City, even if the residents of the free trade zone, out of sheer stubbornness, insisted on calling it a peaceful city, a good show of force with a lot of men put into action could only help to pacify the population. It might even bring in some good publicity for the government. So Operation Free Trade Zone was a symbolic action. Commissioner Frota raised police action almost to a metaphysical level with touches of Greek tragedy. Commissioner Frota had been a fool for not anticipating something like that, especially when some thieves had dared burglarize the house of the Secretary of Public Safety himself, carrying off jewelry, money, a color TV, and a 120-watt stereo.

Before he had changed his colorless name, Alfredo Silva, to the more poetic Catarro, he had been a hefty teenager, sporting black boots, maroon-colored Levi's, a bright Hong Kong shirt and dark glasses. Ever since he had arrived in Manaus, he was the only kid in the whole Japiim neighborhood who wore boots and dark glasses. As far as he knew he really was the only one and for him that was at one and the same time the supreme sign of his integration into the customs of the capital and a clear expression of his manhood. He figured that for his boss, a retired army major who headed up a private security company providing guards for banks and the mansions of the rich, the boots and the dark glasses were perfect because of the arrogant and petulant air they lent him. Even though the major's face always bore a hung-over expression, what Catarro saw behind that chronic-headache grimace was a sign of his own aptitude for wearing boots and dark glasses. Be that as it may, he ended up getting fired one day, boots and dark glasses and all, for sleeping on duty and for stealing the van of the Chinese owner of the import shop he was supposed to be guarding every night. He was furious because of the injustice of it all, not so much for the nickels and dimes he earned to keep his eyes open all night, with his ear glued to a battery radio, listening to the announcer's sentimental drivel and the tear-jerking songs, but more because he had lost the right to pack the 38-caliber Taurus revolver he would spin in his fingers for his drinking buddies in the pool hall. He also felt that without the baby-blue uniform with emblems on the shoulders and his soft leather kepi, he had lost the lawman status that so impressed the girls at the midnight show at the Guarani Theater, who were mesmerized by the karate films and all those little Chinese guys getting it on with the girls. In his uniform he could get it on with the girls too, and in fact it was in the middle of one of those karate films that he met a little woman with long hair and a magnificent set of dentures.

She was a completely off-the-wall girl who always said that God surely wrote in crooked lines, whenever she got in a scrape at the Jungle Whore-house, the liveliest and most violence-prone whorehouse and high altar of nightlife in that red-light district of the Hundred Thousand Whores. She was really a wild lady and ended up making him her sweetheart. She was flaky and liked kissing, even though she had never been kissed in her life. Nobody wanted to kiss a whore, much less one that had false teeth. The first time he got really irritated with her was precisely because of her insistence on kisses, a request he refused, saying he was not such a big fool as to go around kissing toothless streetwalkers. Things had gotten out of hand, even come to blows, and the only reason he didn't thrash her soundly was that the neighbors intervened and separated them. The truth of the matter was that knocking her around seemed to have become a habit, and she seemed to enjoy it. In the Jungle Whorehouse she was known as the Potira Girl, and everybody said she really was an Indian. His beer buddies in the pool hall started to rib him, saying that he had turned into a FUNAI bureaucrat, but he could have cared less, since he had no idea what the FUNAI was.

The Potira Girl had run away from the Salesian School and gotten a job as a worker on one of the shifts at the Sayonara Electronics cassette factory. A job that crushed her spirit entirely. It was a crazy idea for the Potira Girl, with her false teeth, to spend eight hours in a cubicle under fluorescent lights, with two fans stirring up the hot air, between wire-grate partitions, soldering endless transistors onto printed circuits, or adding plastic fasteners to cassette cases. At the end of each shift, all the workers exited through a security check, where they were searched by the guards to be sure they weren't stealing anything. The Potira Girl did not like having any old guard putting his lousy hands on her ass every day just to be sure she hadn't stuck a transistor under her dress. She ended up buying a dress made of Japanese brocade, with a short skirt, and hanging out at the Jungle Club, to which she was invited by a taxi driver, her first client who paid her well. The Potira Girl decided she'd be a fool to go back to her job in the Sayonara Electronics factory, where she was earning a miserable salary each month, just a pittance per day, when in just one night she could pull in the dough hand over fist, earning ten times the fucking salary those sons of bitches were paying her. That's when she ran into Catarro, who had already become a celebrity by trying to filch the billfold of the Papal Nuncio and was working on a deal involving the street kids on Guillerme Moreira Street, who were hawking to the tourists shopping in the import shops, selling things like pirated videotapes, counterfeit Cross ballpoint pens, and a salve to apply to the penis for sexual stimulation. Catarro was getting rich from his business in the free trade zone, profiting on the sale of pens, the aphrodisiac salve, which was actually Vicks Vaporub, and even more from the sale of videos, which were in fact nothing more than a block of wood wrapped in paper with photos snitched from porno magazines. Catarro picked up the salve straight off the ships at next to nothing and sold it for ten times as much as he paid. One of his false porno videos cost thirty cruzeiros, and it was not unusual for a tourist to fall into the trap and to hurriedly hide the incriminating package inside the Samsonite bag he had also just purchased. The Potira Girl thought Catarro was a real cool guy and couldn't understand why he refused to kiss her. Catarro had not had her luck when he arrived in Manaus. So he was a real straight-up kind of guy at first. He'd given her a pair of lemon-yellow panties and let her stay in his house as long as she wanted, even though Bacurau and Miss Free Trade Zone were there ogling her lemon-yellow panties and little cone-shaped breasts.

When Catarro came to Manaus, he had had it with spending sleepless nights, a knife in one hand and a kerosene lantern in the other, keeping an eye on the chicken coop so that no anaconda, those damned snakes that could move with incredible agility, would swim in silently during the night and wreak havoc in his father's flock. Every year it was the same thing, in his father's hut on stilts at the edge of the Cambixe River, a few hours by motorboat from Manaus. Every year the river would rise and invade everything, and they had to hang everything up off the floor and put the animals in cages so they wouldn't drown or be killed by the piranhas, electric eels, or anacondas. His father thought all that was natural, and he never lost any sleep over it. He even thought it was crazy when all those social workers showed up every year, wringing their hands and insisting on giving him shots or money that he figured he didn't need, and trying to convince him that he should build his house on higher ground, where he knew it was absurd to want to live. Catarro had worked hard lugging bananas to the market and later in the Ceasa stacking up crates of oranges until he had enough cash to buy a pair of black boots, dark glasses, and maroon Levi's. But nothing compared with the sheer pleasure of sitting at a table in the pool hall in Japiim, drinking a beer and listening to some good music. And if God really was writing anything, as the Potira Girl kept saying, He must be tracing his most inspired lines, even if they were crooked, at the table in that pool hall.

Commissioner Frota had his jacket open and his Italian tie comfortably loosened and falling over his unbuttoned shirt, revealing a tuft of chest hair, all to show the reporters how exhausted he was after forty-eight hours of his triumphant operation. The reporters could care less about the chest hair and about his fatigue, which, of course, was ungrateful on their parts, thought the Commissioner. But he was sure that the reporters would be keeping their end of the bargain and that the newspapers would, in their similar styles, recount the story of the police action. A reporter friend of his approached and tapped him on the shoulder but drew his hand back in poorly disguised disgust when he realized that the policeman's shirt was soaked with sweat. The reporter was carrying a blank notepad in his hand and was saying that it was crazy the way Catarro had died, in a pool of blood and piss. He also recalled that the Potira Girl had a pair of cone-shaped tits, and that it was just as crazy that she was there spread-eagled, with nothing on but those lemon-yellow panties, riddled with bullets. Commissioner Frota was sure that an operation like this one could be repeated once a year to vary the police routine a little. The reporter looked like a coloring-book Indian, his mouth sarcastic and his yellow eyes showing no sign of intelligence. He was Manaus's most brilliant police reporter, and he wrote real editorials on the police page, lamenting the lack of resources the police had to work with and the benevolence with which the justice system seemed to reward criminals, putting thieves and murderers back on the streets because of stupid technicalities. Whoever read those articles came away thinking that the author was a fellow who enjoyed a good fight and that precisely for that reason was a complete idiot. Commissioner Frota did his best to put on an expression of utter exhaustion, but instead he looked better and healthier by the minute, his sweat dried by the breeze rustling the branches of the papaya tree where an MP was trying to knock down a ripe papaya that had been completely pecked by the birds. The reporter wanted to know if the thieves might not have some connection with the drug trade, and he listened as an angry Commissioner Frota grumbled that they were just two cretins who would never have been accepted, as pack mules or anything else by even the biggest idiot in Colombia.

Commissioner Frota wiped his neck, which by now was completely dry, with his handkerchief, thinking at that moment that he was the most virtuous man alive. The virtue he felt was so vast that it was an abomination that anyone should feel that way. It was like needing to belch and not being able to, so he turned to walk out as the photographers flashed pictures there in the room. Commissioner Frota was thinking how crazy it was that the Potira Girl had a pair of tits shaped like cones and false teeth, not to mention the torn pair of lemon-yellow panties.

Catarro never felt the bullet tear through the flesh of his left thigh; it just felt like a piece of saw grass scratching against his maroon pants, so he didn't even so much as glance down to see the long muddy stain on his pant leg. He was in a hurry to get home and give the Potira Girl a beating, without really knowing why. He tried to take the back steps in one leap and felt a tingling in his rib cage that increased his desire to piss. He was thirsty and went into the kitchen looking for a glass and thinking that it was crazy for the Potira Girl to go around saying that God was writing in crooked lines. She was always saying crazy things, just like a girl, like the time he came out of the Central Police Station, after he'd been beaten up, and she took care of him, rubbing arnica on his bruises and telling him he shouldn't let the cops mistreat him, that he had rights, he was a citizen, even if he was the son of a shore-dweller whose house was flooded every year. He had understood absolutely nothing of what the Potira Girl was telling him and figured she just talked to hear herself talk.

Catarro sat on the kitchen stool, his body leaning to one side, and realized that he was very tired. He couldn't hold the pee any longer and let it run down his leg voluptuously, his leg was burning, his side was burning, and he was sweating like a pig. He allowed a thought to come into his head; it occurred to him that the Potira Girl was a real crazy lady, and that if God was writing all that, it wasn't just that His lines were crooked; the fact was that He had lousy handwriting.

NICOMEDES SUÁREZ-ARAÚZ
Translated by the author

From a book in progress

After a cycle of fifty years, the January rains of 1954 in the savannah grasslands of Bolivia's Amazonia were stronger than ever. At night, I heard my father's angry remarks seemingly directed at the sky. The rains were ceaseless. The snow was melting in the Andes. All that water would continue to feed the green and brown lagoon laying siege to our house and the nearby town of Santa Ana, mingling into a single substance the farm with the forests and inhabited areas, grasslands and mounds.

After rising a yard over the patio of our house and about half a yard inside the bedrooms, the invertebrate body of water became stagnant, shutting down my father's beef jerky factory. The scanty sunlight prevented the meat from drying, and it would rot. My father had the workmen build wooden platforms above the water; narrow bridges made with giant rafters connected the central house to the separate building with the rows of bedrooms, and to another housing the large kitchen with its huge pantry, laden with fruits, vegetables, and canned goods brought on the river boats.

Sleeping became progressively difficult. Vapor rose between the wood planks and created a hothouse effect inside the rooms. Clothes never dried completely. The compound seemed planted in the shimmering water.

Unable to send beef jerky to Rocarol Vassilakis for distribution throughout the Brazilian Amazon towns, my father fretted. His fourteen workmen ambled idly wearing their rubberized ponchos and faces between contentment at being free from work and concern about their own small holdings—their homes and fields of cereals and vegetables. Only a few of them, Yomeye, Raimundo, Castulo, and Domingo, could be employed in attempting to save cattle, particularly the calves. The cattle stood numbed by the water with the glazed look of death in their round eyes, emaciated from lack of food after the first days of the flood. At that rate there would be no money to send even their other two sons Rodolfo and Ito back to La Salle School in Cochabamba. And now my mother, Nina, was speaking of sending a third one.

"We have to send him away," my mother said, referring to me, their youngest child. "He's eight years old, and he hasn't even been taught the multiplication table."

"He'll do fine. When it's time, he'll go," my father said.

"It is time, Nico. He is the only one who hasn't had a chance to go to school, and here he'll turn into a good-for-nothing, what with the drinking and fighting and gambling that goes on in town. He can't stay here. Rodolfo and Ito are in La Salle, and they're getting a solid base. Niquito doesn't even know the alphabet. We've been negligent, Nico. He has to go this year."

"I suppose he can get there swimming."

Refusing to be deterred by my father's sarcasm, my mother continued: "We can catch the steamboat to Trinidad and from there fly to Cochabamba."

At the age of eight I was less concerned with multiplication tables than with perfecting my swimming. This I was able to do in the huge flooded patio between the dorms and the central house of our farm, El Saladero. I hoped the flood lasted forever and I would never have to begin school.

After getting up from bed, I skipped over the bridges and jumped into the water. I could find footing in the shallow water but also ventured beyond the fence that marked the edge of the river. Sardines, *bagres, dorados*, an occasional *pacú*, stingrays, and piranhas—well fed and, therefore, generally inoffensive—swam through the waters of the patio. It was a perfect place for fishing. So with Pedro, the son of one of the workmen, I fished in the patio's water.

To simplify the task of fishing I used a machete to slice fish as they passed by me. I was to find out that a machete leads a different life in water than it does in the air. Live as a sharp electric eel, the machete glided in the water eluding my grasp and swung around hitting me a shade below the tendon of my left foot. It felt instantly hot and a red stain surged to the top. I ran to the nearest bridge six yards away and watched how the piranhas fluttered around the bloodstain. With blood dripping into the water I rushed to lock myself in a corner bedroom, more afraid of my father's recriminations than concerned about the wound. My mother called at the door pleading with me to come out, that I had to be treated. But I remained silent. My left foot trembled; the blood unceasingly flowed out.

"Your father is not going to do anything to you. You have to get cured," my mother pleaded.

The burning sensation increased, but it seemed to be happening to someone else. My mind was gripped by the fear of the repercussions of my foolish act, not by any possibility of my dying. But I remembered the worker who got tetanus from an ax cut and died, and the dread of that possibility won over. I opened the door a crack. My mother pushed her way in and held me by the arm.

"Can you walk?" she asked. I nodded. We edged past the threshold, and there Yomeye, one of El Saladero's workmen, picked me up and carried me to my parents' bedroom and set me on a chair.

"We have to sew him up," my mother whispered with that quiet tone I heard her use when the worker with the ax gash in his foot was lying in his cot bleeding.

My father came in. "Here's some novocaine," he said. "The town doctor, Lorenzo says, has been called to Villa Bella. He won't be back for at least a day." With a movement of the lips he motioned Yomeye to hold me. "This is so it doesn't hurt."

My foot lay under the chair, out of my sight. I felt liquid poured on it; it fizzed. And then something pierced the skin, and I knew that whatever they had injected in my ankle to numb it had not worked, but I wasn't going to complain. I would not die. And I felt the jabs and the odd sensation of my skin being pulled three times. Tears fell between the nook of my thumb and index finger, and I observed the precision with which the tears had hit the exact angle of the folds of the skin.

"He's still bleeding a lot," my mother said. "Tighten the tourniquet, Nico."

"It could cut the blood flow too much. Have him place his foot above his head."

"He can't stay here. If he stays he'll either die accidentally or grow up like your older sons. Brawlers and skirt chasers. He'll have to go with the other two to Cochabamba. He is bright. Grandma Leti says he is the brightest of all of them."

At the long wooden table of the dining room, which could seat up to eighteen people, my mother presiding at the head of the table, and four of their eleven children present, father said that what happened that day to the not-so-bright child of his brought to mind what occurred on July 23 of 1938 to his compadre Eloy Santos, there in the upper Yacuma, just passing the property of the Elsners.

My father's precise memory was his diary. From it he could bring back with date and color and taste sixty years of experiences he had lived and those of many others he had been told about. The date, the temper of the day, the color of a tie, the manner a man had of putting on his hat or drinking from a dry gourd, the spots and ulcers on a leper's arms he had once seen in the deep forest, the size and weight of a fish pulled out by Raimundo, the Brazilian foreman, the day my brother José Pedro brought the French ambassador to visit El Saladero, the weight of the ten heaviest bulls that were slaughtered there and where each one of them came from, the words pronounced at his dying bed by the man who had killed Captain Romero in the port of Santa Ana, the nervous tic and the cataract-invaded eyes of the Uruguayan who sold El Saladero to him in 1945, the regalia uniform of Colonel Pedro Manuel Suárez, his uncle, the day he was officially presented as Ambassador to the Court of St. James in 1908, the day his parents took him for the first time to Manaus to catch the ship that would take him to England, and what each person he had seen wore on the particular day he saw them, what they ate at a certain lunch or dinner, and the internal sequence of many days. And he most vividly remembered what occurred to his compadre Eloy Santos and which he told because he knew that fear was better than death. It kept children in line until they understood for themselves where life ends and death begins.

Often, his anecdotes were told to entertain his guests; that day, however, he broke his rule of never telling sordid stories at mealtimes.

"He was a poor man, Eloy Santos, a small-time farmer, who at every harvest of watermelons and plantains and oranges would drift down the current of the Yacuma to sell his produce. Sometimes he brought firewood, and I would buy it all for the cauldrons where we boil fats.

"He would yoke his two small canoes, tying them up in the old way with a number of cross boards to make more room for loading his produce. That day he was coming with his wife, my comadre Elvira, and their three children. The eldest one, Paco, was seventeen, and the youngest, Elvirita, was fourteen. My godchild was the one in the middle, Edelberto, a little scrawny teenager, kind of freckly. Unusual, because they were both rather dark, but it seems that the grandfather of Elvira had some Swiss blood, probably from one of those men the Casa Suárez brought to Cachuela Esperanza. Now Edelberto lives here in Santa Ana.

"Well, they would often travel by night to avoid the heat, but they did so only on moonlit nights. That time they must've been in a hurry to arrive at Santa Ana for the fiesta because there was no moon and they would not make it to the procession of the first day."

My father paused. With avid yet measured gulps he drank water from a tall crystal glass engraved with his initials: NSF. I also reached for my glass.

Rodolfo, my older brother, sat to the right of Father and was smiling with that derring-do smile his lips set into while he listened to something out of the ordinary, even when he knew the story by heart. Grandmother Leticia looked on with her deep-set eyes from the right side of the table, where I sat next to her. Her piercing green look echoed her daughter's

dreamy green eyes. My mother's low blood pressure became worse when
the weather turned hot, and she was almost dozing off. Father spied at her
with a playful look of complicity with the others at the table.

"Since there was no moon that night, my compadre Eloy told his wife
they should rest, that he would stay awake. He placed a flashlight in the
prow set on a hook on one of the canoes, the left one, I believe, because he
was left-handed. It was one of those flashlights with four batteries, and he
used it to give him an idea of how close the boat was to the banks. He would
raise the long oar off the water but kept it on the hinge and would steer the
boat with a paddle while sitting at the rear of the left canoe.

"The comadre Elvira was asleep when it happened. The crash woke her
up. The boat had hit some overhanging branches. The lamplight was
knocked off. All she heard was the scream, but she couldn't see Eloy.

"'Eloy, Eloy!' she screamed several times, but he only answered back
the first two times. She shouted to her children, who were awake by then,
to look for matches, look for candles, but by then the splashing in the water
sounded no different than the usual gurgling of water currents when they
force their way through branches. One of the kids, Elvirita, found the
matches. They lit three candles, but the water was by then even quieter.
Eloy didn't appear, so my comadre Elvira said: 'Use the pig's tripe. Put it in
the water, and get as many of them as you can.' There must have been a
great sadness in her voice, also the horror of knowing what had happened."

My father paused.

"And they pulled them in, all night until dawn. They had crashed
around eleven at night. Hundreds and hundreds of piranhas, filling up the
long and empty front spaces of both canoes, and two big feed bins carved
out by Eloy and his older son, and which they were bringing to sell. By
mid-morning they had slit open all of them, but they found very little."

He paused again, drinking some more water and readjusting the white
silk throat kerchief he soaked with alcohol. It kept under control his recur-
ring hoarseness, which had begun in childhood and gotten worse with the
thirty-day trips to Acre herding cattle.

"They found only a few pieces of the flesh of my poor compadre Eloy.
They bagged it in a small rubberized sack, like those for carrying fer-
mented manioc flour. It was about a half a pound at the most. With that
they arrived at Santa Ana. Don Nicanor says he had never seen such faces.
They had seen death like very few people will ever see it.

"The kids forgot some of it as they grew up, but my comadre Elvira
never forgot. She spent on his raised tomb what she didn't have. Asked me
for the money to do it. I never asked for it back. She had a tomb built as

though it were for an oversized man. It still stands in the cemetery, next to the large wooden cross, there toward the back. She places flowers on it every day, and every December when the waters begin to rise, because the back of the cemetery is in the lower-lying area, she worries and gets Edelberto, who still lives here in Santa Ana, to take anthill clods and place them around the ornate tomb to make sure the waters never break it open.

"Who knows how she is going to manage to prevent it this summer. José Cholima, who has come from the North, says that they've never seen so much water in their life. And the same is happening downstream. If the waters continue we are going to end up with the biggest flood ever," Father said and looked fixedly out the window.

MILTON HATOUM
Translated by Ellen Doré Watson

From the novel *The Tree of the Seventh Heaven*

The Voice of the Father

My trip ended in a place it would be an exaggeration to call a city. By convention or convenience, its inhabitants insisted on considering it part of Brazil, which seems as arbitrary as the three or four countries within the Amazon region considering an imaginary line through an infinite horizon of trees a border. And here, in this misty jungle unknown even to most Brazilians, my Uncle Hanna had seen combat for the Glory of the Brazilian Republic; he even attained the rank of colonel, while back in Lebanon he had been a sheep farmer and fruit wholesaler to the cities on the southern coast. We never understood why he had gone to Brazil in the first place, but we were amazed and dismayed by his letters, which took months to arrive. They told of devastating epidemics; barbarous acts of cruelty committed with singular finesse by men who worshiped the moon, innumerable battles stained the colors of twilight, men who ate the meat of their own kind as if savoring a leg of lamb, palaces surrounded by splendid gardens and sloping walls with pointed arched windows facing the western sky where the moon of Ramadan appears. They also described the dangers to be braved—rivers so vast their surfaces were endless mirrors, reptiles with iridescent skin brilliant enough to wake him up just as his eyelids were closing at the sacred siesta hour, and a certain poison the natives made no belligerent use of but that, on penetrating the skin, would put a person to sleep and induce terrible dreams, concentrations of pure unhappiness distilled from his or her life.

Eleven years after emigrating to Brazil, probably around 1941, Uncle Hanna sent us two photographs of himself, which were each glued to pieces of cardboard and then glued back to back. The photographs came with a note that said: "There is another picture sealed between the two pieces of cardboard, but it should only be looked at when the next family member arrives here." When my father read this, he looked at me and said: "It's your turn to cross the ocean and explore the unknown on the other side of the earth."

I knew that Manaus was the name of the place where Uncle Hanna lived, and I knew that everyone knew everyone there, that even the most ferocious enemies rubbed elbows occasionally. The journey itself turned out to be very difficult: more than three thousand miles and several weeks long. Sometimes, especially at night, it seemed as though we few adventurous folk on the ship were the only survivors of some catastrophic event. I lost all sense of time. When finally, one intensely hot night, the captain's voice announced we were about to drop anchor just outside the port of Manaus, it was hard to believe we had really arrived anywhere at all. Not a single light was to be seen on the horizon. Above our heads there was a festival of stars, the reflections of which danced on the surface of the river along an endless imaginary line beside the boat; only the darkness between the two proved there was land.

I anxiously awaited daybreak. In spite of its great mystery, nature is almost always punctual here. At five-thirty everything in the invisible world before us was absolutely still; minutes later light dawned like a sudden revelation, tinged with many shades of red like a carpet extending on the horizon, where thousands of sparkling wings appeared: flashes of ruby and pearl. During this brief interval of tenuous luminosity, I noticed an immense tree, roots and crown stretching in opposite directions toward clouds and water, and I felt comforted, imagining that it was the tree of the seventh heaven.

With everyone around me asleep, I witnessed that sunrise alone. It was the most intense I have ever experienced. In time I came to understand that a vision of a singular landscape can change a man's destiny, making him less of a stranger to the land he's about to walk upon for the first time.

Before six o'clock, everything was visible: the sun looked like a single, brilliant eye lost in the blue roof of heaven and, out of what had been a dark stain spreading before the boat, the city was born. It wasn't much bigger than many villages huddled between the mountains of my country, but the fact that the land was flat accentuated the repetition of wooden hut after wooden hut and exaggerated the splendor of the larger stone structures: the church, the military garrison, one or two large private homes in the distance. Needless to say, there were no palaces; those had been inventions of Hanna, the most imaginative of my father's brothers. Back home in our village, a huge leg of lamb served as the stimulus to get him telling a world of stories; the older folks would listen raptly and the blind and deaf patriarch of Tarazubna would interrupt, adding a word or gesture during moments of hesitation, when something was left out.

I stepped off the boat onto a narrow plank and walked through a crowd of people eagerly awaiting news, relatives, or packages. They all seemed to be barefoot, openmouthed, and a little sad. Some looked just plain hungry and there was no hiding it. I searched the crowd for Uncle Hanna, but no one looked anything like him. Finally a tall, beefy young man slouching against a red wall caught my eye. Somehow I found the words in Portuguese to ask him if he happened to know the man in the two-sided picture I held in my hand.

"That's my father," he said solemnly, staring me in the eye and ignoring the photos. I embraced him and asked after Hanna; he merely pointed toward the horizon, where the sunrise was still blazing, and began walking down the only street in the village. Clearly I would be wise to follow. Little by little I realized that the wooden houses lining both sides of the street looked completely deserted; I concluded that their inhabitants were all milling around down at the dock. As I padded along the soft earth after the man who claimed to be Hanna's son, I saw that it must have rained before daybreak (perhaps while I was praying), because not only was the ground soggy but the laundry and foliage were dripping wet. Three hundred yards or so later, the street (and the village) ended. We crossed a rickety wooden bridge over the *igarapé* that separated town from forest.

It had never occurred to me that Hanna might live in the jungle, like an ascetic in the thousand-year-old cedar forests of Lebanon! But it stands to reason that solitude means different things in different places. An almost nocturnal darkness reigned here, and the air was thick on the narrow, tortuous path beneath the trees. I began to have my doubts about the young man who claimed to be Hanna's son and chided myself for having believed him, wondering if I were walking into an ambush. Like anyone in a potentially dangerous situation, I was scared; I considered saying something, or turning around and walking back in the opposite direction, but as I hesitated between alternatives the terrain suddenly changed and a beam of light revealed the end of the path. A kind of clearing up ahead seemed a strange interruption of this shadowy world. I don't know why, but I began staring at first one, then the other picture of Uncle Hanna, flipping the cardboard over in my hand as I walked. The two images, which before had looked identical, now looked somehow different. I imagined this was the result of some chemical change during processing. Two prints from the same plate probably always result in two distinct images, I told myself. I flipped the cardboard nervously in my hands, comparing the two portraits. The gradually improving light emphasized certain slight differences: the curve of the eyebrows, the prominence of the cheekbones, the texture of the hair. The figure of the young man up ahead caught my eye. I stepped out into a flat, treeless clearing of beaten earth, an enormous hole in the jungle.

I didn't need to be told which grave was Uncle Hanna's: the only one without a cross and images of saints. Suddenly I remembered the photograph hidden between the two pieces of cardboard. Ripping them apart, I found another picture of Uncle Hanna, from long ago, before he left Lebanon; but it could just as easily have been his son. I didn't ask for the particulars of Uncle Hanna's death. There was no shortage of possible explanations, after years of living in a place where fevers proliferated as widely as knife wounds. No wonder the cemetery was larger than the village! Neither was I interested in the identity or fate of the boy's mother; I learned later from an acquaintance that she was the best-looking woman around, and that the first words of Portuguese, besides her name, that Uncle Hanna learned were: queen, pearl, marble, star, and moon. Maybe these nouns came to represent her name, dispensing with the need for the complex verb *to fall in love*. It struck me that jealousy might have been what killed him. At any rate, the first time he met a woman the son would begin avenging his father.

I lived in town for a few years. I got to know the most remote rivers and soon learned that, in addition to knowledge of the four arithmetic operations, being a businessman required a certain malevolence, daring, and disrespect, if not disregard, for some of the teachings of the Koran.

Coming to Manaus was my last adventurous impulse. I decided to stay because from a distance the cupola of the Municipal Theater reminded me of a mosque I had never seen in person but remembered clearly from pictures in books read to me when I was a child and from the descriptions of a man I'd known who had made the pilgrimage to Mecca.

I knew I was going to marry Emilie long before Emir disappeared. There were quite a lot of Middle Easterners in Manaus, almost all living in a neighborhood near the port. We Levantines always gravitate to the banks of a river or a coastline, and anywhere we go the waters we see and touch are also those of the Mediterranean. All the bachelors spoke of Emilie with great enthusiasm and hopefulness; the older ones recalled their youth. After all, they had many decades behind them. Emilie was an only daughter, and from all I heard about her I couldn't help falling in love.

HOMERO CARVALHO OLIVA
Translated by Asa Zatz

The Creation

Air, sun, and clouds; river, ravines, and trees; animals, insects, and people. Dawn was breaking, the moistness of the dew muting the sounds of darkness, awakening the denizens of day. The winds departed, following the path of the sun, leaving behind in the town children buried for want of shelter, the earth tendering in death what was denied them in life. Day dawned.

From doorway to doorway, upon this corner and that, people greeting one another, a smile on their lips, hope in their handshakes; the women hugging their children, their warm bodies giving them assurance of good harvests and sunny hours to come. San José awoke in a frenzy of joyousness, the season now under way that holds promise of evenings that unfold when the day's toil is done; the young people would be helping their elders, glances straying, bodies expectant. The men, machetes at the waist, carrying-bags over the shoulder, would be crossing themselves as they passed the church, so old, so neglected that its walls were crumbling away in great patches. They had learned from their parents to make the sign of the cross and knew from them that long before their grandparents were born, a man addressed with fear and respect as *padrecito* used to say mass and perform baptisms and marriages, a man who, the old people told them, taught prayers and forgave sins in the name of God. They spoke, too, of a holy book, the Bible, that contained divine wisdom, and said that its pages held the history of the world and its meaning and revealed what was to come. And, with the words "In the beginning God created heaven and the earth . . ." they recalled to them that God was, and is, the creator of all things. And looking about, they believe, for the earth was prodigal, the heavens providing them water for their crops, the sunlight for their days, and the moonlight for their nights. San José.

"On the first day, God said, "'Let there be light . . .'"

Noon of the first Monday. Month of September. Miguel Guagama, eldest of the men, received notification on the first morning breeze. Arriving on foot with a laden mule in tow, Abraham Afchá stopped before him and, after proffering a courteous greeting, asked where he might rest. The peddler settled down precisely in the spot the old man indicated and, speaking Spanish with the letters twisted around, impressed the people with the excellence of his goods, textiles, and merchandise which he bartered for their weavings. His fascinating talk of faraway lands with great cities that had broad, lighted avenues made a conquest of the youth. On the first Monday of the month of September, on a moonless night, the people all marveled to see beams of light unlike any given out by their tallow candles filtering through the spaces around windows of the house that was turned over to the newcomer. Abraham Afchá, a lantern beside him, was resting, well satisfied with the day's work and dreaming of distant places.

"On the second day, God called the firmament heaven . . ."

The town's dogs were barking everywhere, their howls fading out in the distance with the last rays of the sun, proclaiming a long-awaited return. The man entered San José on the very path by which the peddler had come a month earlier. It was the second Tuesday of October, and the young people recognized him as the omnipotent Lord of whom the old people had told them, who possessed the power to forgive mistakes. He greeted one and all as he entered and, on reaching the ancient church, knelt in the soft earth of San José and prayed. By the next day, men and women were rediscovering the mysteries of the holy scriptures and reaffirming through baptism their faith in Him who dwelt in heaven. Father Andrés Iriarte spoke to them of Christ and asked their help in rebuilding the church. The great doors, sealed until then by fear of the unknown, were thrown open before the priest's astonished eyes. Noting that nothing inside had ever been touched, he was deeply moved.

The pale faces of the European saints conserved the rigidity of their martyrdom unperturbed by the thick spider webs that encircled their heads. And the bas-reliefs, carved in precious woods by the ancestors of these men now gazing in wonderment at the temple's splendor, asserted their magnificence even from beneath the blanket of dust. Not many days later, Father Andrés Iriarte held the first mass in the San José Cathedral, as he had named the church with the presence of heaven and its creator made palpable in his words. Father Andrés, a Spanish cleric, had been sent to the town in view of the interest being aroused by the thousands of head of cattle that grazed free on its fields, owned by nobody.

"On the third day, He separated the land and the seas . . ."

Ignacio Guaji, a man respected in the village for his bravery and uprightness, demonstrated on many occasions which there is no point in recalling here, looked on in puzzlement as three men, recently arrived, set to work busily staking out the ground with landmarks and fencing off large tracts of rice fields and pastures. It was the third Wednesday of the month of November, and the families wondered what was happening, the men commenting that the intruders were saying the land belonged to them, the Salvatierra brothers, by grant from the government at the capital. The three men had arrived mounted on spirited steeds, pistols on their hips, followed by six mules laden with rolls of wire; and they carried papers signed by the prefect, the highest authority in the department, as was verified by Father Andrés at the townspeople's behest. In the light of these events, the elders held a meeting at the conclusion of which Abraham Afchá was appointed to find out, insofar as he was able, what was happening.

"On the fourth day, God ordered the season, the months, and the days ..."

The trader returned on the fourth Thursday of the month of December, mounted this time and bringing goods, but accompanied by ten men in uniform, which made the surprise even greater since the villagers had never seen uniforms before. Afchá called the people together in the town square and addressed them. He reported that the authorities in the capital, concerned with the development of a region as fertile as San José, had decided to keep more closely in touch with the area and, to that end, had delegated full authority to Pedro Román, appointing him mayor and entrusting him with enforcement of the law. Pedro Román, the mayor of San José, a pudgy, bald man, expressed his appreciation for the terms in which he had been honored by "a noble son of this very soil" and proceeded at once to propose that five of the village's sturdiest youths join the ranks of the garrison to don with pride the national uniform and obey orders to the letter as behooves good soldiers; and, in addressing them, he lifted his voice exhorting them to fulfill their duty to the nation. The other man in civilian clothes turned out to be the Chief of Police and also a notary, who would take charge of the legal aspects of land tenure, keep the records of births, marriage, and deaths, and maintain peace and order in the town. Weeks later, in the main square named "General Soandso of the Republic of ..." by the mayor, construction began on what months later was to be the town hall, an imposing building two stories tall.

"On the fifth day, God created the animals that were to inhabit the seas and the land ..."

It was Father Andrés, the man in whom the villagers of San José had placed their trust from the moment he had entered the village, crucifix upon his breast, who confirmed the legality of the documents, counseled the people to work hard in this world in order that they may enjoy divine blessings in the next, and clapping them on the back, headed them toward the haciendas, saying, "Blessed are the poor for they shall inherit the Kingdom of Heaven." On Friday, the fifth day of the third week of January, the lassoers of San José set out for the open fields to rope all the cattle that were grazing free on those lands of God, now under terrestrial ownership as attested to by signed and stamped official paper. And so, those animals descended from the stock abandoned by the Jesuits in the time of the Conquest were driven into temporary stockades prepared weeks beforehand, their new owners' initials to be marked on them later with a red-hot iron. San José, a settlement accustomed to killing only enough for daily sustenance and to letting animals run loose, had to slaughter cattle and deprive them of their freedom in order to feed and clothe themselves, in order that they might live. Converting life itself into a means of livelihood.

"On the sixth day, God created man in His image, in the image of God created He him: male and female created He them ..."

Isidro Male was the father of two beautiful daughters of the type upon whom nature has lavished all its radiance and joie de vivre: two young women, the pride of the town. On the sixth day of the second week of February, Isidro Male awoke at an hour when the un-confessed wander about seeking absolution, his heart rousing him with premonition of tragedy. On Saturday, the sixth day of creation, two of the Salvatierra brothers abducted the town's loveliest women and carried them off, gagged, to El Futuro, a hacienda belonging to Juan, where they were to be violated later in the course of a night of drunken debauchery.

The young men of the village were unable to speak, unable to look one another in the face, for the knots of rage and shame that choked up their throats. Listening to the accusation of the girls' father and the elders, Father Andrés was troubled and promised to see justice done before the day was out.

The moon of the seventh day found him alone and ineffectual, infected, as with the plague, by the rage and shame of the young men.

"On the seventh day, God sanctified and blessed it ..."

On the same path by which Abraham Afchá had arrived a month earlier to sell his wares, now much traveled by peons, peddlers, cowboys, players, government representatives, and others, just at a time when the streetlights were casting strange shadows on the walls, Carlos Morales entered the village, unsaddled his horse, and requested lodging which the parish priest agreed to provide, once satisfied with the traveler's identification of himself as a schoolteacher who had come to settle in the village in question ready to begin work as soon as possible. It was on the seventh day of creation, the last Sunday in March, that Carlos Morales reached San José with his relocation certificate issued by the Ministry of the Interior, his schoolbooks, and an inclination to avoid being killed.

Morales, a native of those humid regions, had been given the certificate of relocation to this remote and prosperous little town in recognition of his participation in demonstrations against the present government and for having cast in his lot with the struggle of his fellows. Abraham Afchá saw him arrive; the Salvatierras observed him from the cantina as he went by. As soon as Pedro Román and the Chief of Police were apprised of the newcomer's presence in San José they rummaged in their files, extracted the pertinent document, and brought it to the cantina where the proprietors of the village met, to take up the matter. Inasmuch as all that the official communication stated was "Carlos Morales, opponent of the government of His Excellency . . . relocated by order of this Ministry in San José where he is required to remain and take charge of the village school . . .," Abraham Afchá, old and canny, recommended close surveillance for the moment and withholding action until such time as the man made a move. This well-taken counsel having been approved, the conspirators withdrew to rest.

On Sunday, the seventh day of creation, Andrés Iriarte, parish priest of San José, was reading the Bible. Having opened it at random to Genesis, book of primeval history, it seemed to him that God had been hasty in sanctifying those twenty-four hours of the seventh day as a time of rest.

Fig. 3. Moacir Andrade. *A lenda da Tocandira* [The Legend of the Tocandira]. 1980. Acrylic on canvas, 110 cm x 80 cm. In the artist's personal collection. By permission of the artist.

Biographies

Authors

Ciro Alegría (1909–1967) was a novelist, short-story writer, and compiler of fables and legends. According to Antonio Cornejo Polar, Alegría is the first classic novelist of Peru, one "who consistently transformed and enriched the tradition of [Spanish American] regional writing." During the 1930s, Alegría participated in the socialist and Indigenist APRA political party and, because of it, was deported to Chile where he lived from 1934 to 1941. His best-known works include *La serpiente de oro* [1935; published in English as *The Golden Serpent,* 1943], *El mundo es ancho y ajeno* [1941; published in English as *Broad and Alien is the World,* 1941], and *Los perros hambrientos* [The Hungry Dogs] (1942). Alegría's short story "La llamada" [The Call] comes from *El sol de los jaguares* [Jaguar Sun], posthumously published in 1980.

Luiz Bacellar (1928–) is one of the most important writers of Brazilian-Amazonian literature. He was born in Manaus and grew up during a time marked by the economic crisis that followed the Rubber Boom. His work is distinguished by erudition at the same time it is touched by themes and motifs of popular culture and the folklore of his birthplace. His work is also infused with an intense musicality. He studied sociology, anthropology, and museum studies. He is a founding member of the influential Clube da Madrugada. He is a journalist as well as a poet and has been an adviser to the Ministry of Culture of the State of Amazonas. He was awarded the Olavo Bilac Prize in Rio de Janeiro for his book *Frauta de barro* [Clay Flute] (1963). His other publications include *Sol de feira* [Sun of the Fair] (1973), *Quatro movimentos* [Four Movements] (1975), and *O Crisântemo de cem pétalos* [Chrysanthemum of a Hundred Petals] (1985), which was coauthored with Roberto Evangelista.

José Balza (1939–) was born in El Delta del Orinoco, Venezuela. He is a novelist, short-story writer and essayist, and winner of his country's 1991 National Prize for Literature. He teaches at the Universidad Central in Caracas. His works include, among others, *Los cuadernos del destierro* [Exile Notebooks] (1960), *Falsas maniobras* [False Maneuvers] (1966), *Memorial* [Memorial] (1977), *Percusión* [Percussion] (1982), *Amante* [Lover] (1983), *La mujer de espaldas* [Woman with Her Back to Us] (1986), *Gestiones* [Transactions] (1992), *Tres ejercicios narrativos* [Three Narrative Exercises] (1992), *Realidad y literatura* [Reality and Literature] (1992), and *Dichos* [Sayings] (1991). The story "La sangre" [Blood] was taken from *Ejercicios narrativos* [Narrative Exercises] (1992).

Anibal Beça (1946–) was born in Manaus, Brazil. He is a poet, composer, and journalist who has contributed to national and international publications. He is a specialist in educational technology and was Director of Productions of the Educational Channel of the State of Amazonas. He also has participated in theater and in the visual arts. He was adviser to the Ministry of Culture of his state. He is a member of UBE, the National Brazilian Writers Union, and the Clube da Madrugada. In 1994 his book *Suíte para os habitantes da noite* [Suite for the Inhabitants of Night] was the winner of the Prêmio Nestlé de Literatura Brasileira. In 1998 his collected poems were published as *Banda de asa* [Edge of Wing]. His publications also include *Convite frugal* [Frugal Invitation] (1966), *Filhos da várzea e outros poemas* [Sons of the Floodplains and Other Poems] (1984), *Itinerário poético da noite desmedida à mínima fratura* [Poetic Itinerary of Boundless Nights and Minimum Fracture] (1987), and *Quem foi ao vento, perdeu o assento* [He Who Goes to the Fair Loses His Chair] (1987). He was the editor of *Marupiara—Antologia de novos poetas do Amazonas* [Marupiara—Anthology of New Poets of the State of Amazonas] (1989).

Violeta Branca (1915–2000) was a poet born in Manaus, Brazil. Her first book, *Ritmos de inquieta alegria* [Rhythms of Restless Joy] (1935), as Tenório Telles notes, evidences aspects of the poetry of the 1930s: an identification with the land, with an Amazonian universe. Stylistically, however, it represents a departure from the preceding formalism. She uses a simple language to create a rhythmic, visual, and lyric poetry. Her second volume of poems, symbolically titled *Reencontro* [Reencounter] (1982), reiterates the themes and motifs as well as the stylistic traits of her earlier book. The poems "Minha lenda" [My Legend] and "Iniciação" [Initiation] were taken from her first book; "Entardecer" [Nightfall], comes from her second one.

Astrid Cabral (1936–) is a poet, critic, short-story writer, and diplomat from Manaus, who made a precocious literary debut with the consecrated *Alameda* in 1963. She is a graduate in neo-Latin literature from the Universidade Federal in Rio and has produced accomplished translations into Portuguese for the Biblioteca de Seleçoes, as well as a rendering of Thoreau's *Walden*. Ms. Cabral has been one of the leading figures in the Amazonian cultural identity recovery movement, and her work frequently promotes environmental awareness. Her poetry has been well received in Brazil, inviting comparisons with masters of the Modernist movement such as Drummond de Andrade and Jorge de Lima.

César Calvo (1940–2000) was born in Iquitos, Peru. He was a journalist, prize-winning poet and novelist, and member of the 1960 Peruvian literary generation. His poetry volumes include *Poemas bajo tierra* [Poems beneath the Earth] (1961), winner of the Poeta Joven de Perú Prize; *El cetro de los jóvenes* [The Scepter of the New Generation] (1967), which won an honorable mention from the Casa de las Américas poetry competition; and *Pedestal para nadie* [A Pedestal for No One] (1975), winner of Peru's Premio Nacional de Fomento de la Cultura. In his writings he identifies with the downtrodden of his land and exalts the struggle for social justice and freedom. Critic Alberto Escobar praises the superb musical and visual qualities of Calvo's poetry. In 1981 Calvo published his creative nonfiction work *Las tres mitades de Ino Moxo* [translated into English as *The Three Halves of Ino Moxo: Teachings of the Wizard of the Upper Amazon*, 1995], passages of which are reprinted in this anthology.

Max Carphentier (1945–) is a poet and short-story writer born in Manaus, Brazil. Presently he is Sub-secretary of the Cultural Ministry of the State of Amazonas. He is a member of the Instituto Geográfico e Histórico do Amazonas, of the Union of Writers of Amazonas (UBE-AM), and of the celebrated Clube da Madrugada. His publications include *Quarta esfera* [The Fourth Sphere] (1975) and *O sermão da selva* [Sermon of the Jungle] (1979), among others.

Homero Carvalho Oliva (1957–) is a fiction writer born in Santa Ana de Yacuma, in the Beni Department of Bolivia. His works include *Biografía de un otoño* [Biography of an Autumn] (1983), *Seres de palabras* [Beings of Words] (1991), *Territorios invadidos* [Invaded Territories] (1993), and *Historias de ángeles y arcángeles* [Stories of Angels and Archangels] (1995). "Creación" [Creation] is part of *Territorios invadidos*. In his prologue to that volume, the Bolivian critic Luis H. Antezana notes that Carvalho's storytelling may be classified, in the concept of Deleuze and Guattari, as "minor literature," one that evades preestablished concepts and centers instead on "details, fragments and represents something akin to a perpetual process of displacements." His stories have been represented in Bolivia's major anthologies and several international anthologies, most recently in *The Fat Man of La Paz* (2000) edited by Rosario Santos.

Julio de la Vega (1924–) is an award-winning poet, novelist, playwright, and journalist born in Santa Cruz de la Sierra, Bolivia. His main works include *Amplificación temática* [Thematic Branching Out] (1975), poems; *Temporada de líquenes* [Season of Lichens] (1960), poems; *Matías el apóstol suplente* [Mathias the Surrogate Apostle] (1971), a novel; *Se acabó la diversión* [The Fun's All Over] (1975), a play; and *La prensa* [The Press] (1982), a play. His works included herein depict the confrontation of man and land: the settler, the conquistador, as well as the myths that fed their lusts; the jungle is viewed as a "promised land" that was to be the scene of *mestizaje*, a mixed culture: ". . . the descendants of the Lion of Iberia / and the Orchid of the jungle / wrote history / on immortal wood . . . / Now in the eye of the jungle the new race sings. . . ."

Jacqueline de Weever (1932–) is a poet and scholar born in Guyana (former British Guiana), who has lived in the Amazonian region of her country. She studied at the University of Pennsylvania and is a professor at CUNY at Brooklyn specializing in Medieval Studies. Her poetry has been published in Guyana in the journal *Kyk-over-al*, and in the United States in several journals, among them *Parnassus Literary Journal, Sensations,* and *San Fernando Poetry Journal.* Her latest scholarly work is *Sheeba's Daughters: Whitening and Demonizing the Saracen Women in Medieval French Epic* (1998).

Elson Farias (1936–) is a poet, essayist, and fiction writer. Among his most important works are *Barro verde* [Green Clay] (1961), *Estações de várzea* [Seasons of the Floodplains] (1966), *Ciclo das aguas* [Cycle of the Waters] (1966), *Dez canções primitivas* [Ten Primitive Songs] (1969), and *Romanceiro* [Ballad Book] (1985). Farias displays an affinity for essential river images and themes from the floodplains where he was raised, redolent of song, water, and earth. Valdemar Cavalcante captured the spirit of the writer thus: "Everything said about the land and about humans, everything referring to life, everything that is reflection and image of the environs and of time, interests the poet, who knows how to bring every element to life and give it essential value, thus tendering a beautiful Amazonian song."

Alfredo Flores (1900–1987) was a diplomat, fiction writer, and journalist born in Santa Cruz de la Sierra, Bolivia. His fiction includes the novels *Quietud de pueblo* [Peaceful Town] (1924) and *La Virgen de las siete calles* [The Virgin of the Seven Street Corner] (1941), a novel of customs that has been reedited many times. The short story included in this selection comes from his book *Desierto verde* [Green Desert] (1933).

Juan Carlos Galeano (1958–) is a poet, translator, and essayist born in the Colombian Amazonian region of the Caquetá. In 1983 he immigrated to the United States, where he teaches literature at Florida State University. His work has appeared in magazines in Latin America, the United States, and Europe. He has contributed to literary journals and newspapers in Colombia, among them *El Tiempo, El Espectador,* and *Revista Casa Silva.* He has published two volumes of poetry, *Baraja inicial* [First Hand] (1986) and *Amazonia* (2003). In 1999 he translated into Spanish and published a selection of poems by Charles Simic. In 2000 his poetry was included in a CD-ROM anthology of Colombian poetry and in *A poesia se encontra na floresta* [A Gathering of Poets in the Amazonian Forest].

Milton Hatoum (1952–) is a short-story writer and novelist. He studied architecture in Brazil and literature in Paris. He is Professor of French Language and Literature at the University of the Amazon in Manaus, Brazil. His publications include two novels: *Relato de um certo oriente* [1989; first published in English as *The Tree of the Seventh Heaven,* 1994; a new edition by Bloomsbury Publishers of England will appear in 2004 with the title *Romance of a Certain Orient*], and *Dois irmãos* [2000; published in English as *The Brothers* in 2002]. His first novel won the Prêmio Jabuti, Brazil's top literary prize. It was also published in translation in French, German, and Italian.

Germán Lequerica Perea (1931–) was born in Iquitos, Peru. He is a poet and short-story writer. His publications include the poetry volume *La búsqueda del alba* [The Quest for Dawn] (1957), from which the selection included in this anthology was excerpted. Luis Hernán Ramírez notes that Lequerica's work "is the symbol of a real and concrete awakening, the final and unyielding protest leading to the definitive liberation of Amazonians" (*Varadero*, 1997). In his poetry there is an intense yet veiled accusation that becomes more direct in his three published collections of short stories: *Ese maldito viento* [That Accursed Wind] (1984), *El viaje de la vida* [Life's Journey] (1986), and *El soplador y el tigre* [The Blower and the Jaguar] (1987).

Erasmo Linhares (1934–) is a short-story writer and journalist born in the municipal district of Coari, State of Amazonas, Brazil. He has been a contributor to important journals and newspapers in Manaus, including *Nossos Dias* and the literary supplement of *O Jornal*. He is a member of the Clube da Madrugada and the União Brasileira de Escritores. His work is included in the collection *Antologia da cultura amazônica* [Anthology of Amazonian Culture] (1970) edited by Carlos Rocque and in *Antologia do novo conto amazonense* [Anthology of New Short Stories from the State of Amazonas] (1971), from which "Beriberi," the story included in this anthology, was taken.

Los Escribanos de Loén is a group of apocryphal sixteenth-century authors, which was created by Nicomedes Suárez-Araúz in the 1960s. The writings of the scribes were presented in a sixteenth-century calligraphic hand. Several Latin American critics, among them the Uruguayan Julio Ricci, assumed these authors to be genuine contributors to the literature of Latin America.

Max Martins (1926–) is a poet born in the State of Pará, in the Brazilian Amazonia. His main works include *O estranho* [Oddness] (1952), *Anti-Retrato* [Anti-Portrait] (1960), *A fala entre parêntesis* [Parenthetical Speech] (1982), and *Caminho de Marahu* [The Road to Marahu] (1983). His collected works from 1952 to 1992 were published in a volume entitled *Não para consolar* [Not to Console] (1992).

Thiago de Mello (1926–) was born in the small city of Barreirinha on the banks of the Brazilian Amazon. He is the best-known living poet from Portuguese-speaking Amazonia. Like Cabral, Farias, and Tufic, he has been a member of the Clube da Madrugada. Much of his poetry is compiled under the title *Vento geral* [Wind from All Directions] (1986). He has translated into Portuguese poetry by Pablo Neruda, Ernesto Cardenal, and other writers that he met while in political exile and as a diplomat. Throughout his life, Thiago de Mello has been an indefatigable advocate for the poor of his land, especially for the rights of children. This identification with the suffering masses of Amazonia has made him a legendary figure. The title of one of his books, *Poesia comprometida com a minha e a tua vida* [Poetry Committed to My Life and to Yours] (1975), expresses the humanistic expansiveness of this writer whom Gilberto Freire proclaimed, on the publication of Thiago's first book, a master poet. Enio Silveira underscored "the fraternal camaraderie" that has characterized his person and work. Thiago himself has epitomized his humanistic credo in verse: "A life always at the service of life / to serve what is worthwhile / is the price of love."

Yenny Muruy Andoque (1969–) was born in the territory of the Andoque tribe that became the reservation called Resguardo Indígena Predio Putumayo in the Department of Amazonas, Colombia. Her indigenous ancestry includes Andoque on her mother's side and Uitoto on her father's side. Muruy knows Spanish as well as the languages of her parents. As a child she studied in the Indian boarding schools in the towns of Araracuara and Leticia. She dedicates herself to the care of her family's fields. She is an expert potter, basket-weaver, and wood-carver, crafts from which she draws inspiration for her poetry. Her work has been published in journals in Leticia.

Raúl Otero Reiche (1906–1976) was a poet, narrator, playwright, professor, and journalist. He was born and died in Santa Cruz de la Sierra, Bolivia. Otero Reiche took part in the Chaco War, composing verses in the trenches, writings that he published in 1935 under the title *Poemas de sangre y lejanía* [Poems of Blood and Distance]. His main works are *Flores para deshojar* [Flowers from Which to Pluck the Petals] (1937), *Semblanza y biografía de Gabriel René Moreno* [Sketch and Biography of Gabriel René Moreno] (1939), *Soledad iluminada* [Illuminated Solitude] (1972), and the posthumous *América y otros poemas* [America and Other Poems] (1977). He was among those responsible for the curious anthology *Los más mejores versos de los más peores poetas de Bolivia* [sic] [The Bestest Poems by the Worstest Poets from Bolivia] (1926).

João de Jesus Paes Loureiro (1939–) is a poet, playwright, essayist, and musician born in Abaetetuba, a city by the banks of the Tocantins River in the State of Pará, Brazil. In 1990 he completed a doctorate in the sociology of culture at the Sorbonne, Paris. He has held several official government positions in the State of Pará; most recently he founded the Instituto de Artes do Pará [The Para Arts Institute], which he directs. He is the author of many collections of poetry, among them *Porantim* (1979), *Deslendário* (1981), and *Altar em chamas* [Burning Altar] (1983), published together as *Cantares amazônicos* [Amazonian Songs]. In 1998 he won the important Prêmio Jabuti for his book *Romance das três flautas* [Romance of the Three Flutes]. According to David Brookshaw in *Paradise Betrayed*, Porantim refers to man and nature as they enter into contact. In Paes Loureiro there is a clear consciousness of myth and song as not only initiatic but transformative acts, as well as the sense of loss of what Mircea Eliade called "mythical time." Invading man precipitates the fall into history, rupture, betrayal, exile: "lost, the time without time, innocence / lost amidst false title deeds, lost / the horizon of the river, the infinite / eternity lost amidst calendars." In 1991 Paes Loureiro produced the important canonical reference *Cultura amazônica—Uma poética do imaginario* [Amazonian Culture: A Poetics of the Imaginary] (1995).

Benjamin Sanches (1915–1978), born in the State of Amazonas, Brazil, was a poet and short-story writer. He contributed to the prestigious Sunday Supplement of the *Jornal do Brasil* and participated actively in the cultural association Clube da Madrugada. His publications include a poetry volume, *Argila* [Potter's Clay] (1963), and a short-story collection, *O outro e outros contos* [The Other and Other Short Stories] (1963). His forgotten work became, in the words of critic Antônio Paulo Graça, "the most eloquent silence in the literature of the State of Amazonas." In 1998 his short-story collection, from which "O estropiado" [The Cripple] was taken, was rescued from oblivion by its re-publication as part of the collection *Resgate* produced by the government of the State of Amazonas and Editora Valer.

Pedro Shimose (1940–) is a poet, essayist, narrator, professor, and journalist. Born in Riberalta, Bolivia, he has long been a contributor of literary, film, and art criticism to such newspapers as *Presencia* in La Paz. At the age of twenty, he won first prize in Bolivia's national poetry competition; in 1972 he won the prestigious Casa de las Américas Prize (Havana, Cuba) for his poetry collection *Quiero escribir pero me sale espuma* [I Want to Write but Only Foam Comes Out]. Pedro Shimose oversaw the "Letras del exilio" [Letters from Exile] collection produced in Spain by Plaza and Janés Publishers. His main works include *Sardonia* (1961), *Poemas para un pueblo* [Poems for a Nation] (1968), *Caducidad del fuego* [Expiring of Fire] (1975), *Reflexiones maquiavélicas* [Machiavellian Reflections] (1982), and *Diccionario de autores iberoamericanos* [Dictionary of Ibero-American Authors] (1982).

Márcio Souza (1946–) is a novelist, short-story writer, playwright, and essayist born in Manaus in the State of Amazonas, Brazil. He has held important government positions, among them the presidency of FUN-ARTE [The National Foundation for the Arts]. Souza is one of the most influential prose writers and cultural identity theorists working in the Portuguese language today. Often making use of the mock-adventure genre to create deft, burlesque allegories, Souza is known for his best-selling novels *Galvez: Imperador do Acre* (1977) [published in English in 1980 as *The Emperor of the Amazon*] and *Mad Maria: romance* (1980) [published in English in 1985], a farce based on the Madeira-Mamoré Railroad project, the most deadly, foolhardy, and futile rubber-era scheme of all. Besides these two novels, others have also been published in English translation, among them *Condolência* [*Death Squeeze*, 1992] and *O fim do terceiro mundo* [*Lost World II: The End of the Third World*, 1993]. His novels have been translated into other languages besides English, and he has won the major literary prizes of Brazil.

Nicomedes Suárez-Araúz (1946–) is a poet, fiction writer, visual artist, and translator born close to the Mamoré River, a tributary of the Amazon River, in Beni, Bolivia. His works include eleven books, among them *Caballo al anochecer* [Horse at Nightfall], which won Bolivia's national 1977 Premio Edición "Franz Tamayo." In 1973 he formulated Amnesis, an Amazonian-inspired aesthetic theory of creative amnesia, praised for its originality by R. Buckminster Fuller, Enrique Lihn, and in J. L. Borges's journal *Proa*. In the 1960s he fabled the apocryphal region of Loén and its sixteenth-century scribes. His work has appeared in Bolivian national anthologies and many international ones including *El Coro: An Anthology of Latino and Latina Poetry* (1997), edited by Martín Espada; in *Oblivion and Stone: An Anthology of Bolivian Writing* (1998), edited by Sandra Reyes; and, translated into Portuguese, in *A poesia se encontra na floresta* [A Gathering of Poets in the Amazonian Forest] (2000), edited by Thiago de Mello.

Sui-Yun (1955–), a poet, journalist, and translator, was born in Iquitos, Peru. Presently she lives in Germany. In 1983 she published *Rosa fálica* [Phallic Rose], a collection that won a Mairena Honorary Mention in Puerto Rico. This book of poetry was published by Les Cahiers du Désert in a French translation by Marcel Hennart. Her latest volume of poetry, *Soy un animal con el misterio de un ángel* [I am an Animal with the Mystery of an Angel], appeared in 2000. Her work has been included in several Peruvian and international anthologies, most recently in *Interkulturelle Literatur in Deutschland* (Metzler Verlag, 2000) and *Inventario relacional de la poesia en español, 1951–2000* (Altorrey Editorial, 2001). The poem "Reportaje a Iquitos" [Report to Iquitos] was taken from *Rosa fálica*. The other poems in this anthology are from the journal *Trocha*, July-August 1993.

Jorge Tufic (1930–) is a poet and essayist from the State of Acre, Brazil. He is the author of several volumes of poetry, among them *Os mitos da criação e outros poemas* [The Myths of Creation and Other Poems] (1980), *Existe uma literatura amazonense?* [Is There Such a Thing as a Literature from the State of Amazonas?], and *Clube da Madrugada: 30 anos* [Clube da Madrugada: 30 Years] (1984). A consummate memorialist, Tufic writes in an intimate, anti-rhetorical style that is deeply imbued with Amazonian myth and legend. His lyrical focus has included explorations of God, country, love, death, nothingness, and identity. A highly allusive and intertextual poet, he believes that poetry serves as a "warning that one ought never to remain indifferent."

Fernando Urbina Rangel (1939–) was born in Pamplona, Colombia. He has been a professor in the Department of Philosophy at the National University of Colombia since 1963. He is the author of three dozen articles and four books: *Mitología amazónica: Cuatro mitos de los Murui-Muinanes* [Amazonian Mythology: Four Myths of the Murui-Muinanes] (1982), *Amazonia: Naturaleza y cultura* [Amazonia: Nature and Culture] (1986), *Las hojas del poder* [Leaves of Power] (1992), and *PalabraObra* [Word-Work] (1995). He has presented eighteen photography exhibits in national and international expositions, both individually and in collaboration. He has also worked on two television and radio series. In 1995 he was awarded the Medalla al Mérito from the National University of Colombia.

Ana Varela Tafur (1963–) was born in Iquitos, Peru. She is the former editor of the journal *Varadero* and the founder of the Cultural Association Urcututu. In 1991 she published *El sol despedazado* [The Shattered Sun] with Percy Vílchez. The same year her poetry volume *Lo que no veo en visiones* [What I Don't See in Visions] won the Quinta Bienal de Poesía COPE, a prestigious literary award in Peru. The poems included in this book are from that volume.

Alcides Werk (1934–) was born in the State of Mato Grosso do Sul, Brazil, and has lived in the State of Amazonas, Brazil, for more than four decades. His publications include four volumes of poetry: *Da noite do rio* [Of the River's Night] (1974), *Trilha dágua* [Water's Trail] (1st edition, 1980, and four subsequent editions), *Poemas escolhidos* [Selected Poems] (1985), *Poems of the Water and the Land* (a bilingual edition published in Manaus) (1987), and *In natura: Poemas para a juventude* [In Nature: Poems for Young Readers] (1999). In 1982 he coedited the anthology *Poetas do Amazonas* [Poets of the State of Amazonas]. Since his first poems, Werk has been passionately dedicated to represent his Amazonian experience, calling attention to the suffering of the poor river dwellers and to the ecological precariousness of his homeland. Time, memory, and the interplay of day and night are central motifs in his work. Tenório Telles notes that Werk's poetic expression is "lyrical and transparent like the currents of the origin of rivers . . . [it] weaves a song of exaltation of provincial life in its solitary simplicity, balanced in a simple, direct language" (2000).

Translators

Angela Ball is a poet and translator born in Ohio. Her poetry has been published in the *New Yorker* and *Ploughshares,* among other journals. She teaches creative writing and literature at the University of Southern Mississippi, where she is an editor for the *Mississippi Review.*

Lindsey Benitz is a Dean of Faculty intern, editorial assistant, and translator at CALC. She earned a bachelor's degree at Smith College with a major in Spanish and Portuguese and a minor in linguistics.

Steven Ford Brown lives in Boston, where he edits the American Poets Profile Series. His criticism, interviews, poetry, and translations have appeared in the *Christian Science Monitor, Harvard Review, International Quarterly, Literary Review, Rolling Stone,* and other publications. Brown is the translator of *Exile: Twenty Poems of Alejandra Pizarnik* (1994) and *Astonishing World: The Selected Poems of Ángel González* (1993). He is completing his translation of *I Never Asked to Be Born a Woman: The Selected Poems of Ana María Fagundo, 1965–1990.*

Alice R. Clemente is a professor emeritus at Smith College and now editor of Gavea-Brown publications at her alma mater, Brown University. She has done many translations from Portuguese and Spanish. Most recently, she edited an anthology translated from the Portuguese, *Sweet Marmalade, Sour Oranges: Contemporary Portuguese Women's Fiction* (1994).

Charles Cutler is a translator, scholar, and professor emeritus of Brazilian and Luso-African literature at Smith College, where he was for many years chairperson of the Spanish and Portuguese Department. He has been coeditor and associate editor of *Amazonian Literary Review*. His translations have appeared in the *Massachusetts Review, Two Lines,* and *An Anthology of Portuguese Writers.*

Frederick H. Fornoff is a professor of Spanish and humanities at the University of Pittsburgh, Johnstown Campus. His translations of Manuel González Prada's *Páginas libres* and other essays were published in 1998 by Oxford University Press as part of the new Columbia University Series of Nineteenth-century Literary Classics. He is a translation consultant for the series Pittsburgh Editions of Latin American Literature at the University of Pittsburgh and a former president of the American Literary Translators Association.

Cola Franzen has translated criticism (*The Challenge of Comparative Literature,* by Claudio Guillén, 1993), poems by Juan Cameron, and several books by Alicia Borinsky, including the novel *Mean Woman* (1993). In 1999 she published the bilingual-format *Horses in the Air and Other Poems/Caballos en el aire y otros poemas* by Jorge Guillén, which won the Harold Morton Landon Translation Award.

Marguerite Itamar Harrison is a translator, scholar, and assistant professor of Portuguese at Smith College. She received her doctorate in Luso-Brazilian literature from Brown University. She is bilingual in Portuguese and English, and her translations of contemporary Brazilian prose have appeared in the journal *Brasil/Brazil.*

Erik L. Iana is the pseudonym used by Erik Olmsted, Ana Olmsted, and R. Kelly Washbourne for their collaborative translations. Ana Santos Olmsted is from Belém do Pará, Brazil, and holds a doctorate in Brazilian literature from the University of Massachusetts at Amherst. Erik Olmsted is pursuing an advanced degree at the University of Massachusetts at Amherst and specializing in translation theory.

Lorie Ishimatsu co-translated from the Portuguese *The Devil's Church and Other Stories* by Machado de Assis. Published by the University of Texas Press, her translation received a Columbia University Translation Center Award. Ishimatsu has translated other works of Brazilian short fiction.

Laura Kennedy, Grace Rugg, and Dan Sheff are students majoring in Spanish at St. Lawrence University in Canton, New York. They undertook their homage to Peruvian poet and novelist César Calvo in a translation workshop directed by Steven F. White.

Clifford E. Landers is a professor of political science at New Jersey City University. His translations from Brazilian Portuguese include novels by Rubem Fonseca, Jorge Amado, João Ubaldo Ribeiro, Patrícia Melo, Jô Soares, Chico Buarque, Paulo Coelho, Marcos Rey, and José de Alencar, as well as shorter fiction by Lima Barreto, Osman Lins, Moacyr Scliar, and Rachel de Queiroz. His *Literary Translation: A Practical Guide* (2001) was published by Multilingual Matters Ltd. He received the Mario Ferreira Award from the Portuguese Language Division of the American Translators Association in 1999.

Alexis Levitin's translations from the Portuguese have appeared in more than two hundred literary magazines, including *Partisan Review, American Poetry Review*, and *Massachusetts Review*, and in more than twenty anthologies, most recently the *Vintage Book of Contemporary World Poetry*. He has published twelve volumes of translations, including works by the Portuguese Eugenio de Andrade and was awarded a Witter Bynner Foundation for Poetry grant to complete an anthology of twentieth-century Portuguese poetry in translation.

Jean R. Longland is a translator whose work for more than thirty years has appeared in such projects as *Selections from Contemporary Portuguese Poetry* (1966); *An Anthology of Twentieth-Century Brazilian Poetry* (1972), edited by Elizabeth Bishop and Emmanuel Brasil; and *The Poetry of Jorge de Sena: A Bilingual Selection* (1980). The poets she has translated include Manuel Bandeira, Carlos Drummond de Andrade, and Haroldo de

Campos. She has served as curator emeritus of the library at the Hispanic Society of America in New York City.

Angela McEwan is a writer and literary translator who lives in Whittier, California. She has translated poetry by Lydia Vélez-Román, Verónica Miranda, and Carlota Caulfield. Other translations include a short story by Julieta Pinto, "The Blue Fish." Her own published work includes short stories and essays.

Delia Poey holds a doctorate in literature from Louisiana State University and teaches at Florida State University. She is the coeditor of *Iguana Dreams: New Latino Fiction, Little Havana Blues,* and editor and translator of *Out of the Mirrored Garden: Short Fiction by Latin American Women.*

José Manuel Rodeiro is an award-winning visual artist and a translator. He holds a doctorate in comparative arts from Ohio University. He received a Fulbright Fellowship in 1995 and was awarded an NEH grant in 1986 and a Cintas Fellowship in 1982. Presently, he is a professor of art history at New Jersey City University. He has translated Nicolas Guillén, Pablo Neruda, Nicomedes Suárez-Araúz, and other authors.

George R. Shivers was born and educated in Salisbury, Maryland, and completed his doctorate in Spanish and Spanish American Literature at the University of Maryland, College Park. He has contributed articles on contemporary Spanish American fiction to several journals and has published translations of works by Chilean writer Ariel Dorfman as well as poetry by Mário de Andrade and Carlos Drummond de Andrade.

Nicomedes Austin Suárez is a journalist and translator. He studied at Bowdoin College and the University of Massachusetts. He has lived in Bolivia's Amazonia, in Spain, and in Florence, Italy.

Nicomedes Suárez-Araúz's translations have been published in *American Poetry Review,* the *Nation,* the *Norton Anthology of World Poetry,* and the *Massachusetts Review.* He co-translated *Twenty-Four Conversations with Borges* (1984).

Kenneth A. Symington, the translator of César Calvo's *Ino Moxo,* is a researcher of plants that have a history of ritual or shamamic use. During a visit to Tarapoto, Peru, he came upon Calvo's book and decided to translate it. Inner Traditions of Rochester, Vermont, published it in 1995.

R. Kelly Washbourne has published translations in cultural theory by Antonio Benítez-Rojo (Cuba) and Roberto Schwarz (Brazil). His translation of J. V. Lastarria's *Recuerdos literarios* (2000) was published by Oxford University Press. He is at work on the first bilingual anthology of Spanish American *Modernismo*. Since the fall of 2003, he has been an assistant professor at Kent State University's Institute for Applied Linguistics.

Ellen Doré Watson has published several volumes of poetry and translations. She is an editor of the *Massachusetts Review* and has been director of the Poetry Center at Smith College since 1999. Her translations include novels by Márcio Souza and *The Tree of the Seventh Heaven* (1994) by Milton Hatoum.

Asa Zatz began his translating career in Mexico with the translation of *The Children of Sánchez* by Oscar Lewis. Zatz has translated nearly one hundred books and book-length works including the works of Cardoza y Aragón, Carpentier, Eloy Martínez, José Luis González, García Márquez, Ibargüengoitia, Sábato, B. Traven, Valenzuela, Valle-Inclán, Vargas Llosa, and a book of poetry by the Mexican Efraín Bartolomé. He has just completed an Argentine novel for W. W. Norton and is completing *Recuerdos de provincia* by Sarmiento for Oxford University Press.